Henry Nitchie Cobb

Far Hence

A Budget of Letters from our Mission Fields in Asia

Henry Nitchie Cobb

Far Hence
A Budget of Letters from our Mission Fields in Asia

ISBN/EAN: 9783744757218

Printed in Europe, USA, Canada, Australia, Japan

Cover: Foto ©Lupo / pixelio.de

More available books at **www.hansebooks.com**

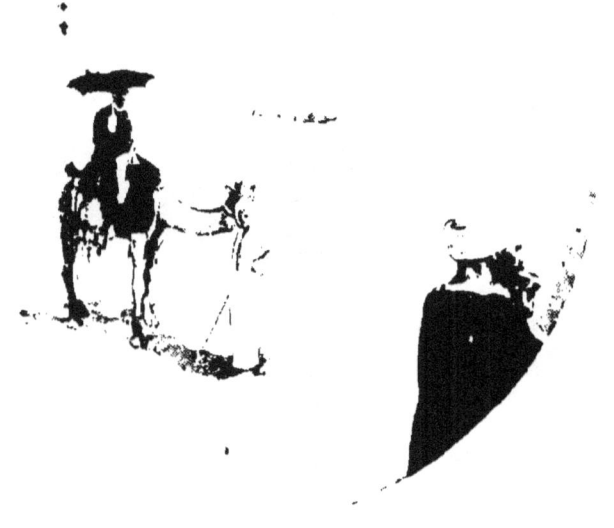

IN THE DESERT

A BUDGET OF LETTERS FROM OUR MISSION FIELDS IN ASIA

BY

HENRY N. COBB, D.D.

PUBLISHED BY
WOMAN'S BOARD OF FOREIGN MISSIONS, R. C. A.
25 EAST 22D STREET, NEW YORK

Copyrighted 1893, by the Woman's Board of Foreign Missions, R. C. A.

AUTHOR'S NOTE.

It was never the intention or expectation of the writer that the letters contained in this volume should see the light otherwise than in the columns of the *Christian Intelligencer*, in which they originally appeared. Hastily written, as a running record of a tour made with a specific object in view and with certain definite limitations, they have seemed to him too narrow in their scope and incomplete in contents, to afford matter of general interest. He does not otherwise view them now. But it has been so strongly represented to him that their publication in their present form might be of use in increasing among our churches the interest felt in our missions in Asia, and the desire for such publication has been so often and so kindly expressed, that he has no choice but freely to yield his own judgment to that of others who are entitled to and have his highest regard. Especially is this true of the Woman's Board, at whose request they are given to the press. Had he the necessary time they should have been subjected to careful revision and enlargement. But he has not. Such as they were originally they must remain, and are here presented. If the Lord shall own them, in any small degree, for the advancement of His work, the importance, success and blessedness of which have grown upon him immeasurably by reason of the experiences which they record, the writer will be more than satisfied.

H. N. C.

INSCRIPTION.

To those ladies of the Woman's Board of Foreign Missions of the Reformed Church in America, whose generous kindness made the journey recorded in them possible, these letters are gratefully inscribed.

INTRODUCTION.

"AND when this epistle is read among you, cause that it be read also in the church of the Laodiceans, and that ye likewise read the epistle from Laodicea.—Col. iv, 16.

Our New Testament would have been much smaller if it had not been the habit of the apostle to write letters to the churches and the disciples, and it would have been larger by at least one letter had not the letter to the Laodiceans been lost.

This little book binds together some letters written to all our churches. Those who have already read the letters, will the more value the volume that collects them. Those who have not, will find them a literature of much significance to our Reformed Churches.

They are the word sent back to us by our Secretary from our mission stations in foreign lands, while he was visiting among them. Upon him daily had come, for many years, the care of all these churches, and to go to visit them, to see the workers at their work, to see the fruit of their toil and the needs of their days, has given him words for us that will quicken our sense of their need of us together with him.

We feel, perhaps, had we passed on the road to Jericho the man "wounded and bleeding and half dead," we would have acted the part of the Good Samaritan. But we forget it was not inhumanity, that made the priest and the Levite cross to the other side, but the *prejudices* of an *unenlightened religious education*. They had passed by the teaching of "judgment and mercy and the love of God," and so they passed by the man who had fallen among thieves.

INTRODUCTION.

A thoughtful knowledge in the minds of those who are called Christians, of the *mission* of Christianity in the world, would keep us from such blind passing by of the needs of men and women and from an unsympathetic neglect of those who are working for them.

May these letters bring so vividly to us the work of those who are bringing the "Gospel to them that are bound" that our part in furthering the work will be done with more heartiness and hopefulness than ever before. Work for the world! That Christianity of to-day may appear better in the eyes of the future, than Judaism in the parable of the Good Samaritan.   M. B. L.

CONTENTS.

		PAGE
Introduction		5

CHAPTER.
I.	Cairo and the Khedive	7
II.	The Mission and the Mosque	11
III.	Aden and the Arabian Mission	16
IV.	Bombay and the Parsees	22
V.	Welcome to the Arcot Field	29
VI.	The Arcot Classis and Mission, and Work at Arni	34
VII.	Station and Village Work	39
VIII.	Vellore Town, Temple and Schools	44
IX.	Among the Hills	50
X.	Coonoor to Palmaner, and the Theological Seminary	55
XI.	Madanapalle, by way of Punganoor	59
XII.	Among the Telugu Villages	64
XIII.	Chittoor, Katpadi and Arcot	68
XIV.	Old Arcot, and the Gudiyatam Conference	76
XV.	Silent Preachers	83
XVI.	Madura Temples and Mission	88
XVII.	Pleasing Prospects in Ceylon	97
XVIII.	Missions and Mountain Views at Kandy	103
XIX.	Tropical Seas and Scenes	108
XX.	A Flying Visit to Canton	117
XXI.	Mission Homes and Schools in China	124
XXII.	Up the Lun River by Sail and Pole	134
XXIII.	Homes, Hospitals and Hospitality at Sio-Khe	145
XXIV.	Amoy Streets, Sights, Sounds and Smells	155
XXV.	The Amoy Churches	163

CONTENTS.

CHAPTER.		PAGE
XXVI.	Among the Chinese Christians	169
XXVII.	Churches, Towns and Temples on Amoy Island	176
XXVIII.	Welcome to Japan and Ferris Seminary	185
XXIX.	By Rail to Tokyo and the Meiji Gakuin	191
XXX.	Beautiful Nikko, and thence to Sendai	198
XXXI.	Matsushima and Morioka	206
XXXII.	Glimpses of Tokyo	214
XXXIII.	Kobe, the Inland Sea and Nagasaki	223
XXXIV.	Kyoto, the Western Capital	232
XXXV.	Last Look at Yokohama	241

FAR HENCE

A Budget of Letters from our Mission Fields in Asia

CHAPTER I.

CAIRO AND THE KHEDIVE.

Dear Friends at Home: CAIRO, January 16, 1892

REASON would, perhaps, that I should have written you before. But the conditions of our hurried trip across Europe have hardly been favorable to correspondence. Had I written you from London, I fear my letter would have been surcharged with the gloom and cheerlessness of one of the heaviest of "black fogs" which that unhappy city has known for years. London weather is rarely of the best at any time. A fine day in London, Emerson declared in his "English Traits," to be "like looking up a chimney," which may, perhaps, have been somewhat slanderous. "A foul day," says the same authority, "is like looking down a chimney," and that is the simple truth concerning a "black fog." For a week the whole city sat, if not in sackcloth and ashes, in darkness and soot. Day was turned into night. Gas and electric lights failed to dispel or even greatly to illuminate the gloom. One hardly dared venture abroad for fear of getting lost. The eyes and throat smarted with the sulphurous vapors with which the fog was charged, and black soot sat on everything. The smoky atmosphere penetrated and filled the houses and churches. Under such gloomy auspices Christmas came and went, and not till the following Sunday did the sun shine, nor was it possible to see across the street.

Even sunny France and Northern Italy were infested with fog, and the latter covered with snow. A letter from Turin, or Venice or Bologna, had it reflected our physical condition, would have given you the "shivers." In fact, all Italy was shivering, as far down as Rome and even Naples. Of two glorious days only, one in Venice and the other in Rome, could it be possible to speak with "warmth."

How different is Cairo! Here the sun shines warm on streets and houses. Here the trees are all in leaf and the roses in full bloom. To live is a delight, and to look out upon the crowds that fill the streets and squares an experience never to be forgotten. Such a commingling of races, such a variety of color and costume it is not possible to see elsewhere except, perhaps, in Constantinople. Those who remain here any length of time become enamored of the life and climate. To stray travelers like ourselves they are simply and supremely fascinating.

We have been fortunate in the time of our advent. The late Khedive, Tewfik Pacha, died, as you are aware, on the 7th. His son and heir, Abbas Pacha, now Abbas II., was absent at school in Austria, and this is the earliest day on which he could reach the capital. So from early morning the city has been all agog. That air of suppressed excitement which betokens the expectancy of some great event was everywhere manifest. The signs of mourning which were to be seen two days ago have disappeared, and decorations and waving banners in honor of the new sovereign are the order of the day. "The king is dead. Long live the king." The streets are filled to overflowing with excited throngs, especially those through which the royal procession is to pass. All Cairo is abroad. The hurrying to and fro of mounted couriers, and officers splendid in gold lace and embroidery, the passing of detachments of troops, of carriages bearing officials and dignitaries or ladies of high degree, with their gayly ornamented *saices* or runners clearing the way, all add to the excitement and brilliancy of the spectacle.

Word comes that the "Ferdinand Maximilian," bearing the hope of Egypt, has arrived at Alexandria at about eight o'clock A. M., and that the new Khedive may be expected in Cairo at two o'clock. The railroad station has been made brave with decorations of garlands and exotic plants, while a sumptuous carpet is spread for the royal feet to tread upon. Before the station are drawn up detachments of Egyptian and English troops, while similar detachments are posted in the square fronting the Abdin Palace, whither the sovereign is to be escorted. As the hour of his arrival approaches, the crowd settles down into comparative quietness upon the streets, so far as movement is concerned. But the noise of their voices is literally "like the sound of many waters" as it comes to our ears. It is itself a spectacle to admire; not like the dense and sombre crowd of an Occidental city, but variegated and lit up with all the colors of the Orient. It is an orderly crowd, too. Though it is estimated that at least 100,000 people witnessed the procession, so excellent were the provisions made and so admirable the conduct of the people, that no disorders occurred.

Prompt to the minute, the guns at the station announced the arrival of the Khedival train, and were immediately answered by the guns at the royal palace. Expectation stood on tiptoe. Soon three lancers opened the way, followed at short intervals by companies of mounted troops. Then, in an open barouche, drawn by six splendid horses and accompanied by twelve Kavasses all splendid in purple and gold, came the young man himself, in whom all interest centered and toward whom all eyes were turned. Answering with his right hand the salutes and acclamations with which he was greeted, be bore modestly and well the ordeal and the honors. His appearance is prepossessing, and his whole conduct since the death of his father has won high encomiums. His appearance would indicate more years than the seventeen with which he is credited. As he passed on, the enthusiasm of the people passed all bounds, and hundreds broke from the crowd, filled the spaces between the carriage and the guard of honor before and behind, dancing, shouting, clapping their hands and singing, moving along with the procession till it reached the palace. Then he dismounted and entered, and ceremonies of presentation, etc., took place, to which the public were not admitted.

The new Khedive is well spoken of, both for his conduct and proficiency in the studies he has pursued, and had made himself very popular among his comrades by his kindly and unassuming manners. On the way to Cairo he is said to have made many inquiries as to the condition of the country and people, the progress of agriculture, methods of irrigation, etc. In short, he seems to have made a very favorable impression.

There is an ugly rumor current to-night that, just before he entered the palace he was shot at, and that two Arabs were cut down by the police for this attempt upon his life. This is ascribed to the fact that he is understood to be very much in love with the English people, and favorable to the continuance of the English occupation. I have not been able to verify the rumor, however, and doubt its correctness. But how little to be envied is he, who, in his youth, comes to the throne with such perplexity and burdensome problems as now confront him, to reign over an impoverished people.

CHAPTER II.

THE MISSION AND THE MOSQUE.

RED SEA, S. S. "Oceana," January 23

We were obliged to leave Cairo a day earlier than we expected, in order to catch the P. & O. steamer for Bombay, for which, however, we had to wait a long eighteen hours at Ismailia. Some of our observations and experiences at Cairo may still be of interest.

The Mission of the United Presbyterian Church is in a very prosperous condition, and it was exceedingly gratifying to visit its excellent school and come in contact with its workers. Their main building is admirably located, in the very centre of the new "Ismailiyeh" quarter, near the principal hotels, and very close to the fine garden of the Esbekiyeh. It occupies the whole of a block or square, which came into possession of the mission in a remarkable and Providential way, as related to me by Dr. Watson.

The mission had formerly possessed a site and building at the end of the Muski street, to which, however, they had no legal title. A former Khedive, desirous of making some improvements, found this school in his way and sought to purchase it. His first offer was of £1,000, which was at once refused. After prolonged negotiations he was finally induced to raise the amount to £7,000, which was accepted ; but the mission found themselves without a local habitation. They intimated to the Khedive that while they might, if they chose, take his money and return to America with it, they had no such desire. They wished to have a school and a place to put it, and as they had given up their old site to gratify him, he ought to give them a new one. This he finally did, and the mission are now in possession, with full legal title, of their present admirable location as the gift of the Khedive. On it they have erected a fine stone building at a cost of $85,000, almost the entire sum having been raised in Cairo by Drs. Lansing and Watson, and the building erected under their direct and personal superintendence. It is a monument to their Christian zeal, patient industry, rigid economy and wise foresight. In it are housed not only the families of the missionaries living in Cairo, but the Girls' School and the Theological Seminary. A fine chapel and large school and class-rooms are also included within its walls. It was my privilege to attend the Sunday-school last Sunday morning, visit some of the classes, and go up with them into the chapel for the Arabic service, and also to be present at the opening exercises of the day-school on Monday morning. The missionaries whom we met, Messrs. Watson and Giffen and their wives, were kindness itself, but we were unfortunate in not being able to meet Dr. Lansing, who was up the Nile.

Beside the services at this centre, others are held at different points in Cairo on Sunday afternoon, while Cairo itself is but one of several important stations, Alexandria, Assioot, Luxor and Monsoora, occupied by this old and successful mission. After thirty-seven years of faithful labor, it now has 286 workers, 108 schools, with 6,696 scholars, 131 preaching places, 109 Sunday-schools with 4,421 scholars, 29 organized congregations with 3,155 communicants and an average Sabbath attendance of over 6,000. The total amount paid by natives in 1891 was $26,321. This appears to include not only their contributions, but also tuition fees and proceeds from the sale of books.

It was cheering to come into contact with such a work.

An intelligent young gentleman whom I met at the school informed me that he and nearly all his fellow employees in the post-office at Cairo had received their education there, "and, best of all," he added, "was the knowledge of God." Yet last evening, on the deck of this steamer, a gentleman from New York, now on his way round the world, confided to me his conviction that missionaries were doing nothing, and could do nothing among these Eastern peoples, rehashing a number of the trashy stories every traveler hears, to their discredit. "Did you see any mission work in Cairo?" I asked him. "Why, no I didn't know there was any there." When I related to him what I had myself seen, he expressed great surprise, and promised that in visiting the principal cities of India and China he would make it his business to inquire for and examine into such mission work as might be found there. It is from just such "intelligent observations" of "unprejudiced travelers" that impressions go abroad, and are by many gladly received, that missionaries are doing nothing, and their pretended work is a failure.

The Mohammedan University in the Mosque El-Azhar is separated from the American Mission by a considerable distance. A far larger interval separates them as to their objects and character. As the latter is the chief centre from which the light of Christian truth is being disseminated throughout Egypt, the former is the most important university and centre of propagation of Islam in the Mohammedan world.

The mosque itself, though ancient, has little about it that is specially interesting or attractive. In fact, like some old churches in Europe, it is so built about by houses, on narrow streets, that it is impossible to get any considerable view of the exterior. We found the interior, also, in a state of great and unprepossessing confusion, as the great court is undergoing extensive repairs. Bricks and blocks of stone and sticks of timber lay strewn all over it, and workmen were busily engaged. These operations, however, did not interfere, apparently, with the work of study or instruction.

The mosque is said to have been converted into a university in the year 378 of the Hegira (the Mohammedan era), or 975-6 A. D. To it students gather from every Mohammedan country. Special sections or colonnades are set apart for the students from different countries, or the different provinces of Egypt. There seems to be no limit as to age, and none as to the length of time during which study may be pursued. We noticed boys of hardly eight years sitting by the side of gray-bearded men, rocking back and forth and repeating audibly the lessons they were committing. A universal hum or buzz pervaded the entire building, which would be fatal to study, were study a matter of *thought*. It is rather a matter of memory—committing by rote—which is, perhaps, facilitated by audible utterance. The teachers go from class to class, or sit on the floor amid their students, and lecture to them or read aloud from books placed on desks before them.

The seventeen corridors include spaces for Turks (from the northern part of the Turkish Empire), Syrians, Persians, Indians and those from various parts of Egypt, Arabia and Africa. The attendant who accompanied us, jealously watching lest the inevitable and irrepressible Kodak should get in its work, against which we had been warned at the gate, informed us in answer to inquiry that when the classes were full there were 12,000 students. This was probably an exaggeration, intended to magnify the importance of the school in the eyes of the unbeliever. Certainly there were not half that number present on the day of our visit, nor is it easy to see how so many could be accommodated. Nevertheless, the number must be very large, and there can be no question of the zeal of instructors or instructed.

The course of instruction embraces no vestige of Western or modern literature, learning or science, but is confined exclusively to the sacred language (Arabic) books and doctrines of El-Islam. Great as the influence of the university is, and must continue to be for a long time to come, its learning and wisdom are yet things of the past, and doomed to disappear at length before the spirit of progress and the Word and Spirit of Christ.

I wish I had time to tell you of all the events in the delightful week spent in Cairo; of our visit to Heliopolis, to the Citadel, of the day spent in the desert visiting the Sphinx and the Pyramids, the largest of which, Cheops, the more adventurous spirits of our party climbed, being rewarded by a most magnificent and unique view. On one side the dreary waste of desert sands; on the other, beautiful Cairo with its Citadel, its mosques and minarets—but I must not linger.

CHAPTER III.

ADEN AND THE ARABIAN MISSION.

P. & O. S. S. "Thames," January 26

The "Oceana," on which we embarked at Ismailia, was bound for Australia. This made necessary a transfer at Aden to the Bombay steamer on which we are now ploughing the Arabian Sea. The dire tales of the extreme heat on the Red Sea, with which our ears had been filled, were all falsified in fact, and our experience has been delightful in the highest degree. The officers of both vessels assure us that we have been favored with an unusually cool season. An English Admiral on board has contrived to manufacture a grievance out of this freak, or turn, of fortune, declaring that he has made the voyage many times, and never found it so cool before. Now there is not heat enough (79 deg. F.) to enable him to get up his accustomed thirst! Needless to say that his disappointment is one with which we hardly sympathize, though the barkeeper may.

The sea, too, has been and still is calm and quiet, and but for the beautiful blue and broad expanse of water, it would be easy to fancy ourselves on the surface of the Hudson on a warm summer afternoon. The appearance of land, of which we have had but few glimpses, however, is sufficient at once to dispel such an illusion. The green slopes, and wooded heights, the thriving towns and smiling villages are wanting. The barrenness of ragged rocks, sharp and jagged steeps, or sterile deserts without a trace of human habitation, is all that met our eyes till we came to Aden. Nor even there was there any green thing to be seen.

STREET SCENE—ADEN INDIA.

Scarcely had we dropped anchor in the outer harbor, at 9 o'clock yesterday morning, when the tall form and smiling face of our good brother, the Rev. S. M. Zwemer, of the Arabian Mission, appeared on deck, and hands were firmly grasped in cordial greeting. It was a pleasure we had been looking forward to and should have been most sorry to miss—only marred by the absence of his comrade, Brother Cantine, who is now in Busrah. After careful examination of various points, these brethren have decided to establish themselves at that place, and Brother Cantine has now been there some weeks. Thither Brother Zwemer expects to turn his steps in a day or two, having kindly delayed his departure on our account. With such slight knowledge as I have of all the facts in the case, it, of course, becomes me to speak with caution. But a glance at the map would seem to show that Busrah possesses considerable advantages for a new and successful mission. At the head of the Persian Gulf, within easy access by boat of a large population along the Arabian coast and in the valleys of the Euphrates and Tigris. being also in communication with the outside world, yet with no missionaries located there, by whom their coming might be regarded as an intrusion, their choice would seem to be a wise one. As a place of residence I should judge it to be preferable to Aden, where the climate in hot weather (as I was assured by a junior officer of the "Thames") "has only a sheet of brown paper between it and ——."

It was cheering to find our brother in good health and cheerful spirit, to note his courage and interest in the work and people, and the readiness with which he is already able to communicate with them. It was also pleasant, and characteristic of the man, to learn that his interest has not been confined to the native residents— Arabs, Somalis, Swahilis, etc., of whose kindliness and freedom from bigotry he spoke emphatically—but that he has also engaged in labors for the spiritual welfare of the British garrison stationed here. Denied the use of the English chapel by the chaplain, he pointed out to us the humble building in which he was accustomed to hold meetings with the soldiers, where they "had a delightful meeting last night, and expect to have another to-night." To them, doubtless, his departure will be a loss.

The Keith-Falconer Mission was pointed out to us, lying some six miles to the north of the city, and now occupied by two missionaries only. The location has proved unhealthy, being exposed to pestilential fevers, to which the noble and lamented founder fell a victim but six months after his arrival. This, and the mission composed of Brothers Cantine and Zwemer—four persons altogether—comprise, I believe, all the missionary force at present engaged among the millions of Arabia. It was with great satisfaction that I learned that the Committee at home have promised them additional laborers and also a boat. A medical missionary would seem to be almost indispensable.

There being several hours at our disposal before the sailing of the "Thames," we gladly accepted Brother Zwemer's invitation to go ashore and visit the city of Aden.

It may not be generally known that the rocky promontory on which this city stands, as well as the surrounding country for a score or more of miles, is a British possession and a constituent part of the government of India. The rocks are plainly of volcanic origin, and are thrown up into all sorts of fantastic shapes. The British have crowned many of the summits with fortifications bristling with guns, pointing in every direction, landward and seaward, constructed military roads, tunnels and underground passages, and are fast making, if they have not already made, of it a second Gibraltar. There is always a British regiment here, besides artillery and a contingent of native troops. The town itself and Steamer Point, where vessels land their goods and passengers, are strongly policed, and good order maintained, as everywhere under British rule.

Yet even policemen in uniform find it impossible to control the importunities of "gharri" drivers, Jewish money-changers, merchant venders and beggars who dog the footsteps of the wondering, wearied and at last disgusted traveller. Thankful for the presence of our guide, we committed ourselves with the most implicit confidence to his direction, and set out for land and the city of Aden.

This city of 40,000 inhabitants (by the last census) lies in the crater of an extinct volcano, completely shut in by jagged peaks and ragged slopes, where the heat of summer must be awful, and is entirely invisible from the sea. The high wall of rock which hides it from view is scarred and seamed, and dotted here and there with caves, in which fugitives from justice often seek to hide themselves, and are taken. One of these caves, high up on the mountain side, its opening partly walled in by light colored stones, is pointed out as the grave of Cain, the Mohammedans of the place firmly believing that that first murderer was buried there.

As we advance along the fine macadamized road built by the government, the way to the city leads through a narrow and deep defile cut through the solid rock, barred by gates and massive walls, all strongly fortified. Once through and on the inner side, the city of flat-roofed, one-storied houses, dazzlingly white, lay before us, spreading out and nearly covering a somewhat extended plain, while on every side the wall of the crater towered above.

It was a striking spectacle not soon to be forgotten. Nor less so the narrow streets, the swarms of men, women and children of many races, mostly black and half-clad—many with only a cloth about their loins, and not a few of the children in nature's garb alone. The latter thronged about our "gharri," ran after us, beset us on every hand, begging in every possible attitude and with every possible grimace and intonation, for "bakshish." Their patience was worthy of a better cause and larger success.

Two objects of special interest engaged our attention. The one, a series of stupendous tanks, built in a gorge of the mountain, one above another, of massive masonry, and designed to collect for use whatever rain may fall on the summit or higher slopes. Once in about three years they are filled. At present they are dry. Their origin dates far back in the past. Whether they are older than the Roman occupation is uncertain but probable. The Turks found them and repaired them, and the English have recently done the same. Two banyan trees and a few shrubs were growing here, the only ones we saw.

The other object which attracted our special interest was the depository of the British and Foreign Bible Society. The agent in charge, Mr. Ibrahim Abd-el-Masiah, received us very courteously and cordially, and we were shown the various forms of the sacred volume there on sale. It was a surprise to learn that actual sales were made, to unsolicited purchasers, of more than 4,000 copies and portions of the Scriptures last year. One Mohammedan bought 42 copies for use as a text-book in his school in a neighboring village. Every day, men who have bought and read the Scriptures come back and seek further light on them from the agent. One edition of the New Testament, gotten up and bound in the same style as the Koran, is said to be exceedingly popular. Here, in close proximity to the dried-up tanks, was opened a flowing fountain of living, not stagnant water, which, please God, shall never go dry.

But it was needful to return to the steamer, which would not wait beyond the appointed time. There, on the deck, we bade farewell to our dear brother, he sending his salutations to those whom we hope to meet in the Missions of our Church, and we commending him and his comrade to God and the Word of His grace. As our good ship weighed anchor and turned her prow toward India, we left him in the rapidly-increasing distance, alone, yet not alone. For has he not the promise, "Lo, I am with you alway?"

CHAPTER IV.

BOMBAY AND THE PARSEES.

BOMBAY, February 2

We reached Bombay on Sunday morning, January 31st, and cast anchor in the harbor just as the sun was rising over the eastern hills. The harbor, which is one of the finest in the world, presented at that hour a beautiful spectacle, studded with islands of which some rise to a considerable height, flanked on the North and East by mountains, and on the West by the long stretching city, its smooth surface bearing a large number of ships of war all clad in white, numerous merchant steamers and innumerable native crafts, both large and small, with their peculiar, sharp pointed sails. A pleasurable excitement accompanied our landing, as we touched for the first time the soil of India, and came face to face with heathenism pure and unrelieved.

Not that Bombay is a heathen city exclusively or chiefly. But here the old and the new, the heathen and the Christian, stand side by side, blended and yet distinct, and while Europeans abound, yet the great multitudes which throng the streets and oppress one with the sense of their vast numbers are as purely heathen as though Christianity had never come among them and the presence and dominion of Great Britain were unknown. It is a most impressive and affecting sight—the constant streams that throng and almost block the various streets of the native town, dark in hue and dark in mind and heart.

The city derives its name from the island on which it is situated, and which it has greatly outgrown. In fact, it covers several, connected with each other and the mainland by causeways and railway viaducts, and is, in shape, not altogether unlike New York, a peninsula lying north and south, "all long and no wide." It is like New York, too, or Manhattan Island, in its original cheapness, its first cost to the East India Company being an annual rental of ten pounds sterling. Next to Calcutta, which it is fast approaching in size, it is the largest city in India, having a population somewhere between 800,000 and 900,000. There are two very distinct portions into which it is divided : The Fort, or European portion, and the native town.

The Fort is a very handsome quarter, with wide streets, shaded with noble trees, broad squares and esplanade, and a collection of fine buildings such as would do credit to any city in Europe or America. The most conspicuous of these, and perhaps the most elegant, is the Victoria Railway station, which is said to have cost a million and a half of dollars and is truly imperial in style and proportions. It does not put out of contenance, however, the University buildings with their lofty tower, the high court, postoffice, several schools and many other public buildings, as well as private, which abound and beautify the city. A marked feature, in this regard, is the number of hospitals, erected for the most part by private munificence, among which is to be noted the Cama Hospital for Women on the esplanade, and under the exclusive management and charge of medical women. With this is connected an admirable Female Dispensary on one of the great thoroughfares and near the public market. It is a satisfaction to know that the idea of these institutions, as well as the " Medical Women for India Fund," by means of which so much good has been and is yet to be accomplished, had its origin with one of our fellow-countrymen, George A. Kittredge, Esq., long a resident of Bombay. To him, also, is due the introduction of tramways or street railroads, which are now an established feature of the city's locomotion. In both instances Yankee pluck and perseverance triumphed over great indifference and much opposition.

Noticeable among the other buildings is the Crawford Market, the like of which I have never seen anywhere. A large and imposing building of stone and brick at the corner, is flanked on either side and at a right angle by long courts or sheds, along which are arranged, in parallel rows, the benches or counters on which innumerable dealers sit with their stock of vegetables, fruits and other wares exposed. These open on a garden shaded with trees and beautiful with flowers, where venders of birds, monkeys and other animals have their booths, while a third side is enclosed by the markets for meat and fish. Everything is kept scrupulously clean, and in the early morning the entire space is thronged with crowds of chaffering purchasers, the whole presenting a singularly bright and animated scene.

But the native town is by far the most interesting to the visitor, newly arrived from other lands. Even the principal streets are close and narrow, and lined on either hand by the small native shops which give them the appearance of prolonged bazars. In each the dealer sits cross-legged or on his knees, his stock of wares about him and usually within reach of his hand. Every sort of merchandise is exposed in them, from the native wares and food products to the fabrics, both cheap and costly, and even the books of Europe. Treasures in gems and brass and silver work, embroidery, shawls, etc., are here to be found if one knows where to look for them, and to be purchased if one knows how to buy. Such a thing as a fixed price is unknown—at least for foreigners—and unless the would-be purchaser is skilled in chaffering and cautious in bidding, the chances are ten to one that he will be most egregiously "sold."

The crowds that throng these streets are simply immense, interminable. A carriage threads its way through them with the greatest difficulty, and only by dint of incessant shouting on the part of the driver. To turn out seems the last thing thought of, and one often holds his breath in anticipation of a collision that seems inevitable but never comes. Fully half the people have no other dress than a cloth round the waist, their bare backs glistening in the sun and the bare legs exposed. The sight at first is rather repulsive, but one becomes accustomed to it of necessity, as to many another disagreeable thing in this life. But the gay costumes of the other half relieve the sombre monotony of black skins, showing every variety of style and color known to the Orient. Nothing seems to relieve the expression of either dullness or sadness which seems all pervasive. The gay chatter of the French, or the merry laugh so characteristic of the Southern negroes in America are wanting altogether, and the masses in their unimpressiveness become oppressive.

The native houses which line these streets rise to the height of three and four stories, sometimes more, and are decorated with all the colors of the rainbow. The overhanging porches and doorways often display rich carving and betoken the wealth of the builder or possessor. Here, also, in rows, are the Jain temples, gay with many colors, but looking dark and squalid within. At night when the shops are lighted and the crowds, if possible, larger than ever, the sight is singularly impressive and fascinating.

In the heart of this native quarter, Byculla, is located the Mission of the American Board. We had the pleasure of attending a native service on Sunday afternoon, listening to a sermon in Marathi by one of the native preachers and joining, with the heart if not altogether with the understanding, in the songs of praise of the native church. After the service was concluded, some of the young men of the congregation took their stand, according to custom, on the steps of the church. With the aid of songs and musical instruments a crowd was soon gathered and the Gospel preached to them. It was a privilege, in company with another American clergyman from Minneapolis who was passing through, to be permitted to give, through an interpreter, a word of testimony and invitation. The crowd listened intently while the foreigners were speaking and their words interpreted. Who knows but some single seed then dropped, if not more, may take root and grow and bear fruit. God grant it for His Son's sake. The next day we visited the schools for boys and girls, under the care of Rev. J. E. Abbott and Miss Millard respectively, and also the "Bowker Home" or dormitory for the latter school. Their work extends far beyond the limits of the city, and is connected with that of other stations in the Marathi Mission.

A visit to Bombay would be incomplete without seeing the "Caves of Elephanta" and the "Towers of Silence." The latter are situated on the summit, the finest part of Malabar Hill, which overlooks the city. A beautiful drive along the Back Bay makes gradual ascent, passing some of the finest residences of Europeans. With the pure sea air ever blowing, and grounds laid out with taste and beauty, and abounding in luxuriant foliage of tree and shrub and vine, there seemed a trace of Paradise in these hillside homes. The views from them, of city, harbor and mountains are superb. The "Towers" are, as is well known, the burying places of the Parsees, or rather the places for the disposal of their dead—for they do not bury. There are four towers surrounded by high walls, into which no foot of any other than a Parsee is ever admitted. The grounds about them, however, are open to those who obtain cards of admission from the proper source. They are laid out in walks and beds of flowers and kept neat and clean. On entering the great gate of the enclosure one is first shown the hall where the body is deposited while the appropriate service is rendered.

A model of the interior of the towers is shown, displaying a central pit, round which are arranged benches, in three concentric tiers, rising one above the other. On the outer and larger of these are deposited the bodies of men, of women on the second, next interior and lower, and of children on the third. When the body is laid down the friends withdraw and the door is closed. Then the vast flock of vultures, that darken the air with their wings and make it hideous with their cries, rush down upon it. When their repast is finished, and the bones are clean, they are gathered up and thrown into the central pit. We were so fortunate—or otherwise—as to arrive just as a burial party was leaving. The edge of one of the large towers was crowned with a circle of the rapacious birds, sitting in solemn silence looking down into the pit, while a few were flitting uneasily about, flapping their wings and calling to their fellows. On the walls of the other large tower not a bird was to be seen. In answer to our inquiry, the aged keeper said they were all down inside. The mental picture of what they were doing there made us turn away with a sickened feeling, which the sight of the great city and the busy world outside did not at once remove.

The "Caves of Elephanta," on an island of that name in the harbor, are reached by boat, and a visit to them forms a pleasant afternoon excursion. From the landing one ascends up a flight of massive stone steps to a level perhaps 200 feet above the sea. There, cut into the solid rock, is a large temple, in various chambers, with gigantic statues of Hindu divinities in various attitudes and forms of manifestation. Many of these statues have been sadly mutilated, not so much by the ravages of time as by the ignorant hatred for idolatry of the early Portuguese discoverers, and the later vandalism of British soldiers. At present the government guards what remains and maintains a keeper. The grotesque figures, dimly lighted halls and chambers, and the immense masses of overhanging rock, make a peculiar impression of wonder, awe, but hardly of solemnity. They are monuments of the faith and industry of a generation that wrought and died centuries ago, and of a system of superstition that is destined, please God, to pass away before as many more centuries have flown.

CHAPTER V.

WELCOME TO THE ARCOT FIELD.

ARNI, February 11.

We left Bombay on the evening of the 3d, much wondering why the only train for Madras should leave at 9.30 P. M. The reason became apparent the next day, when riding over the hot plains of the interior in the scorching heat. Far better to spend two nights and one day on the road than two days and one night. For the nights are comparatively cool, but the day! too hot even to sleep, and with little that is interesting to distract the attention and relieve the monotony of the long and dreary ride. The sun had done its work, even if the last monsoon had failed to do its. And the ground looked parched and barren, and weary men and women toiled hopelessly in fields that promised little in return. Where the plough scratched the soil the dust flew in clouds. The sun beat relentlessly on the shapeless piles of rocks, bare and gray and glistening, that reared their heads, often in most fantastic shapes that seemed the work of human or titanic hands, and glared back at us savagely, reflecting the heat with which they were themselves tormented.

But all things earthly have an end, and in the cool of the morning of the 5th, at 3.45, we left the train, after a ride of seven hundred miles, and met the hearty welcome and embrace of Dr Chamberlain, who had come all the way from Arni to meet us and escort us thither. The lack of hotels for the entertainment of travellers in most Indian towns has given occasion for provision, at the larger stations, of bedrooms and bath-rooms and other conveniences. So here, at Renigunta, where the South India taps the Madras railway, after greetings were exchanged, we washed away in great bath-tubs the dust and something of the heat of the long journey, and went forth refreshed to begin the circuit of the Arcot district and the stations of our Mission. By invitation of the Rev. Mr. Petersen and his wife, of the Hermannsburg Lutheran Mission, we stopped for breakfast at Tirupati, about an hour's ride from Renigunta.

Tirupati is one of the most noted centres of Hindu worship and superstition. It has many small temples of its own and within its limits. But the chief attraction is a sacred temple on the summit of a mountain which overlooks the town. The path to it leads up through three large "gopurams," or gate towers, standing at intervals on the mountain-side. Through them pilgrims are constantly ascending and descending, and at certain times hundreds of thousands march in procession across the lowland, climb the weary way and pay their devotions and their tribute at the sacred shrine where Shiva's footprint is to be seen imprinted in the solid rock. Few foreigners, indeed, if any, have ever been able to penetrate to it, and whoever makes the attempt does so at the peril of his life. It is just at the base of this mountain, and across the path that leads up to it, that our German brethren have planted and maintain the standard of the Cross. Faith can look forward and anticipate the time when the multitudes shall flock to it. In the face of present tokens it requires a strong faith, indeed, to do it. But the beginning has been made. The mission bungalows, the church, the schools, all of which we were glad to visit, have in them "the promise and potency" of mighty changes yet to be effected in the name and by the power of Him for whom they stand. It was a pleasure to begin our journeyings through our own mission field, by breaking bread in the house of one of another name and race, but of " like precious faith," and who represents the society founded by that apostolic man, Pastor Harms, of Hermannsburg. May his spirit animate all those who go forth under its care.

In reaching Arni we take a new branch of the South India railway, which runs the entire length and traverses diagonally almost the whole width of the Arcot field, bringing, with the exception of Palmaner, all the stations into more or less direct railway communication. When one considers that some of these stations were previously thirty, and even sixty, miles from a railway, and the laborious modes of travel where railways do not exist (of which these letters may have occasion to speak hereafter), it is easy to understand how great this new convenience is, and how great an advantage it is likely to prove in carrying on the work. Had the mission been asked to lay it out, it could hardly have served them better. By 5 P. M. it brought us to Kalambur, the station nearest to Arni, and seven miles only from this place. All along the way we were met, at Pakala, Chittoor, Vellore, by helpers, already friends and brethren, going as we were to Arni.

For here the Mission is holding its annual meeting, deferred two weeks in order that the secretary might be present, and made the occasion of a more general gathering of the helpers than usual because of his expected presence. The good ladies who sent him forth could not have anticipated—as he certainly did not—the universal interest this visit has awakened among the native brethren and churches. If, in recounting some of the experiences through which we have passed, and shall yet pass, the pronoun of the first person shall seem to be used rather too frequently, please remember and believe that it is not from egotism, but simply because it is only possible so to give any idea of this interest, the expression of which found its natural objective point in the secretary and her who accompanied him.

Of this interest the first marked expression greeted us as we passed through the town of Arni and drew near the Mission Compound. Drawn up across the road, dressed mostly in white, was a large company of schoolboys, church members and helpers, with music of fiddle, fife and drum, who immediately formed in line and preceded us to the Compound. At starting, and at frequent intervals on the way, were given "Three cheers for our secretary," and at the gate we passed under a canopy inscribed on its outward face, "Welcome to the Rev. H. N. Cobb, D. D., Our Secretary." The cheers were emphasized by the explosion of fireworks, and continued till we had reached the Mission House, and grasped the extended hands of the beloved brethren and sisters waiting to receive us. Here they were dismissed —for the present only, as it afterward appeared. For the next day, at noon, the sounds of music were heard again, and a large company approached, filling the spacious verandah of the bungalow, bearing garlands of fragrant flowers with which to adorn the visitors. When quiet was obtained an address in excellent English, of which copies in English and Tamil were distributed, printed on the Arcot Mission Press by the scholars of the Industrial school—was admirably read by one of the teachers. It was followed by the presentation of a plate of brass, mounted on velvet, and engraved by an artist of the place, as a memento of the occasion. To this address the secretary, taken completely by surprise, made such reply as he was able. Nor did the manifestations cease with this. For on the following Monday evening the scholars of the school claimed the occasion as their own, and celebrated it with high spirits and right good will, with fireworks, manual exercises, music and song, under the bright moonlight, which here seems to shine with sevenfold brilliance. It was altogether an enchanting scene, and one that will long linger in the memory.

The gathering of helpers here is an encouraging and stimulating sight. As one looks into their faces he cannot help feeling that the Lord has enabled the Mission to raise up a noble band of men, from whom much faithful and efficient service may be expected. Not all are equally gifted or equally equipped. But some of the older men especially—some of the younger also—seem to be men of intellect, spirituality and power. A prayer-meeting was held early Saturday morning, ably led by Pastor Abraham Muni, of Yehamur. The little church was full, down to the very door, with an interested and attentive company. At the close of the meeting an opportunity was given for the secretary to speak, which he willingly embraced, though never longing in his life so much for the gift of tongues as then. It is not easy to express one's feeling or communicate his thought through an interpreter. Joseph Cook calls him "an interrupter," and such he is, however admirably in other respects he may perform his part. He interrupts the course of thought, and—what is more important still—the tide of emotion, which will not flow by jerks and spurts. Nevertheless, the secretary rejoiced in the opportunity to express his own pent-up feeling, as well as to convey to the assembled brethren the warm Christian salutations of the churches at home, as committed to him especially by the Pastor's Association on the day before he embarked.

CHAPTER VI.

THE ARCOT CLASSIS AND MISSION, AND WORK AT ARNI.

TINDIVANAM, February 13.

IN the afternoon the Classis of Arcot met. The opening sermon was preached by Pastor P. Souri, of Madanapalle, and though the absence of the gift of "the interpretation of tongues" was equally deplored, it needed no such gift and no interpreter to enable one to see the fire and force of his utterance or mark its effect on those who listened. The sight of him and his eight brethren in the pastorate, clad in their gowns of spotless white, was one worth going far to see. The session continued through the afternoon, and was resumed the following Monday. On this day were examined for licensure seven young men, the first class which has passed through the entire course of instruction in the theological seminary. They all produced their professorial certificates, and were then examined by Pastor Moses Nathaniel and Drs. Jared Scudder and Chamberlain, and the examination of all was sustained. It was a new step in the progress of the Church in India, as evidenced by the fact that the formula for licentiates had to be written now, for the first time, for these young men to sign. There are those among them from whom, if God shall spare their lives, the Church may yet expect to hear a good account. Those who have founded or maintained the scholarships by which they have been supported, may well thank God for the privilege of being His instruments in putting them into the ministry. And it is to be hoped that more of the churches of the Mission will covet the privilege of having such men as their pastors. The present number, nine, is an encouraging advance upon the past, when for many years there were only three. But there are still fifteen out of the twenty-three churches of the Classis (the Church of Madanapalle has two) without pastors. The great obstacles to the establishment of the relation have been, first, the lack of suitable men, and second, the great poverty of the people. On this point I may have something to say at another time. So long as their condition is unimproved, and the Mission requires (as it very properly does) that a certain proportion of the salary should be paid or pledged by the church before a pastor can be ordained, the increase in their number must of necessity be slow. Nevertheless, continual effort is made to bring them up to the point of partial self-support. The first difficulty is happily disappearing, and must tend to disappear eventually altogether, through the work of the theological seminary.

Of the Mission meetings, held very continuously on Tuesday, Wednesday and Thursday, sometimes, it must be confessed, almost to the point of exhaustion, there is little space and I can hardly trust myself to speak. Suffice it to say, that it was both a privilege and a revelation to be permitted to attend them. The Church may confidently trust that its far-away interests are most carefully guarded by those to whom they are committed. If these brethren, with their complete knowledge of the field, its growth and wants, and with their careful scrutiny of every estimate and every item of expenditure, make up their minds to ask for more missionaries and larger means for any department of work, they ought to have them. They know too well the difficulty with which both are procured to make extravagant or unreasonable demands, if, indeed, any demands could be extravagant for such a field and for the multitudes embraced in it.

The work at Arni has, beside those features which it

possesses in common with other stations, such as a station church, village churches and schools, and caste girls' schools, the intermediate department, called "lower secondary," in the new government system, of the Arcot Academy or High School, and in connection with it the Industrial School. The scholars, numbering now about seventy, are in both schools at once, spending part of the day in study and part in manual labor. Schools of an industrial character are regarded with special favor by the government, which is disposed to foster them by considerable grants. The advantages claimed for the method pursued at Arni are, that it provides active employment for the boys, puts in their hands the means of gaining a livelihood independently of the Mission and its service, which will be of great advantage to any who may prove incapable of promotion to the higher department of the school at Arcot, and it serves to teach them all that work is honorable and idleness and helplessness disgraceful. Blacksmithing, rug-making, carpentering and printing are successfully carried on, and from all the departments creditable and remunerative work has been turned out. The most popular branch is carpentering, which has some thirty boys or more. The whole enterprise is confessedly an experiment as yet, but one that gives promise of excellent results in the future, and is, therefore, well worth trying. The boys look bright, intelligent and happy, with few exceptions, and are interesting also as the nursery from which future helpers, teachers and pastors are to be looked for.

But space fails, and I have not yet even mentioned the various meetings—the communion service on Sunday morning, conducted in Tamil and English, in which all participated and drew very near to one another and to heaven, and at which six lads from the boarding school were received to the communion of the church

COOLIES EATING RICE—INDIA.

—the Sunday-schools in the afternoon, where prizes were distributed to many a happy child, and in one of which many heathen men and women stood looking on and listening, while the lips of heathen children of high caste spoke and sang the words and praise of Jesus Christ, or those caste schools on which Mrs. Scudder expends so much careful thought and labor. Of each and all and more, I would gladly speak if I had time and you had patience. The whole week has been full of interest and pleasure. The hospitable bungalow, aided by no less hospitable tents beneath the palms, has been filled with as happy, harmonious and devoted a company of men and women, I verily believe, as were ever got together, and the privilege of being with them is enough to make one glad for life.

The Mission meeting at Arni broke up at the unseasonable hour of 1.45 A. M. of the 12th. By 5 A. M. we were again stirring in order to take the train for Tindivanam at 7.05. We bade adieu, with regret, to our bountiful host and hostess, the Rev. and Mrs. E. C. Scudder, Jr., their beautiful compound and hospitable home. The drive of seven miles to the station in the early morning was very delightful.

Tindivanam lies on the main line of the South India Railway, about seventy-five miles from Madras, and is the most southern station of the Mission, as well as one of the most important as regards extent of field and the number of villages dependent on it. The station was formerly at Gingee, a fortified town some twenty or twenty-five miles to the west, but the unhealthfulness of that place caused its transfer to Tindivanam.

On our way thither, by a somewhat circuitous route, we passed through two considerable centres of Hinduism, Tiruvannamalai (shortened to Tirunomaly) and Tirucoilur. The shrine at the former place is the special object of superstitious devotion. It lies at the base of a considerable hill or mountain. We counted seven large "gopurams" or temple towers, with several smaller ones. Once a year hundreds of thousands gather at this place from all quarters with their offerings, and march in procession around the temple and the mountain which overlooks the town. Large quantities of rice, ghee (or melted butter) and other offerings are carried up and deposited in a great pile upon the summit. At night the pile is fired, while fires are also kindled on all the surrounding hills, amid the acclamations of the multitudes shouting and calling on the god "Govinda," to whom the shrine is sacred.

To this feast go companies of missionaries and Christian preachers, proclaiming to these worshippers the Gospel of our Lord. It seems a hardy undertaking, requiring strong conviction, great zeal and boldness mixed with discretion. Last year much opposition was manifested by the agents of the Hindu Tract Society, and at their instigation. But these did not succeed in suppressing the preaching of the truth, though manifesting their impotent rage against it. This society is, in itself and its operations, a most emphatic testimony to the effects produced by missionary effort, and to the value and efficiency of the methods employed. For it has copied those methods of preaching, establishing schools, and circulating tracts and books (teeming with misrepresentation and abuse of Christ and Christians), and their utterances are the cry of fear, if not of despair, as well as of hate. Their influence and their activity are already waning. Similar feasts are held at other places prominent in Hindu worship, as Mailam and Conjeveram, both in the field belonging to this station, and both furnishing occasion for the preaching of Christ to the assembled multitudes.

CHAPTER VII.

STATION AND VILLAGE WORK.

TINDIVANAM, February 15.

We reached Tindivanam about noon. Driving up the main bazar street of the town, it was a cheering sight, amid all the dingy squalor of the shops and houses, and after passing several Hindu shrines grimy with smoke and dirt, to come face to face with the pretty new church of pure white, recently built by Dr. John Scudder. It stands at the parting of the ways, in more senses than one, and looks down the long street in front of it as though inviting all the numerous passers to enter and hear the words of life, and looking forward to the day when they shall flow unto it.

Beyond it lie the school buildings and the former missionary bungalow, where the primary department of the Arcot High School is domiciled. Beyond it still, in a new and spacious Compound, gleams the new white bungalow in which Dr. and Mrs. John Scudder have, with their daughter, their happy and comfortable home. It is no longer necessary to put up umbrellas when it rains! As we entered the Compound gate the helpers and schoolboys greeted us with music and song, and, under a canopy of "Welcome," escorted us to the door. Their welcome was renewed the following afternoon, with addresses, garlands and gifts, and the explosion of fireworks, lasting a full half-hour, to the evident delight of the participants. So fully did they enter into the spirit of the occasion, that after being dismissed, they retired to the schoolhouse grounds, and for hours afterward the sound of music and happy voices singing their native Christian lyrics was heard on the night air. One's heart could not but warm toward the singers. It was a pleasure to assure them, as in every place, of the sympathy and Christian affection of those who had sent us and their missionaries to them, and also to preach the Gospel to them on the following Sabbath morning in the church.

We had, on Sabbath afternoon, returning from the Tamil service, an affecting illustration of the besotted superstition in the midst of which our missionaries labor. The catechist of the station, Sebastian, had some weeks before gone to a neighboring village with a cart to bring home some goods. In order to balance the load he had picked up a stone by the wayside, and placed it in the cart. On reaching the village he removed the stone, and threw it down by the side of the street. It was in cholera time, and the people were much exercised by fear of that dread disease. (How they are ever free from it is the wonder—not, that many die). What was his surprise, a few days after, to find that the people of that part of the village had set up this stone as an idol, and were worshipping it. Naturally remonstrating, he told them how it came there, and how foolish it was to think that worship paid to such an object could do them any good. "Ah," they said, "we know that you are a good man, and even if the stone came here as you say, some good may come to us from it."

On the Sunday afternoon we came upon the spot. A wicker booth had been erected over it. Three bricks were set on end on either side of the stone, and all sprinkled with a certain yellow powder used in worship. Before this assemblage of divinities were one or two other stones—servants to the gods—and, as offerings, a little rice and a few bananas. Before the booth, on her knees, and paying her devotions, was a gray-haired woman, wrinkled and skinny with age, and perhaps with want. She rose on our approach, and on being remonstrated with for worshipping such an object, waxed quite eloquent in her own and its defence. "It cannot see, it cannot hear, it cannot speak. Why do you pray to it?" "And did you ever see your God? And did you ever hear Him speak?" This and much more, with much impassioned gesture, and in shrill and earnest tones, was her reply. Poor creature. We left her with hearts sad for her, and for the many, many millions who know no more than she of the true God and eternal life.

It was part of the programme for Tindivanam that we should see something of the village work. As Dr. John Scudder was about to begin his periodic circuit, the village of Orattur was chosen for a visit by the Secretary. Here Pastor Paul Bailey lives, a tall, fine-looking, patriarchal man, with white hair and beard contrasting strangely with the dark hue of his face. By faithful effort he has gathered a church of about eighty members, while fully two-thirds of the people in the part of the village in which he lives are counted as adherents. He has also reared a commodious church building of singular proportions—about fifteen feet by sixty, to which he is now seeking to add a tower in which to place the bell provided by the liberality of friends in Flatbush. The bell at present stands in a corner of the church, and when rung for service—as it was while we were in it—the din and clangor can be better imagined than described. We reached the village, going part of the way by rail and part in Dr. Scudder's buggy, which had been sent on before. As we approached, the heavens, which had been so long shut up, opened and let down, for a quarter of an hour or more, a copious shower. It was accepted as a happy omen, and did not, in the least, affect the ardor of the villagers, who came trooping forth to meet us and escort us in.

Arrived at the church, we descended and found pitched within, in the far end, the beds on which we were to pass the night. (The church is generally, in these villages, not only the best, but the only comfortable sleeping place to be obtained). After getting fairly settled, the bell, with almost deafening clamor, summoned the people to assemble. It was proposed to celebrate the Lord's Supper with them. As they came in they took their seats upon the floor—the men and women on different sides—till almost the entire space was covered to the very door. The surroundings were not such as would be edifying to a congregation of refined tastes. But the service was none the less—rather, all the more—touching on that account. The upturned faces of many, intently drinking in every word, made strong though mute appeal to one's deepest Christian sympathy. Lambs in the midst of wolves, though rude and uncultivated, they were yet Christ's. And that means much where all around are Vishnu's or Shiva's—or the devil's— and hate that holy name by which they are called.

After the service was concluded we walked through the Paracherry — the portion of the village occupied by Pariahs—led by Pastor Paul and escorted by a goodly share of the congregation. We visited the pastor's house and the old church, disused since the new and larger one was built. A low, dark building, of mud walls and earthern floor, of hardly one-fourth the size of the new one. Yet such are the little churches in many of these villages, the one in which we had worshipped being exceptionally large and fine. The Christian houses were pointed out to us, low and dark, with walls of earth and roof of thatch, yet far better than many villages we have seen in our wanderings. Here and there we stopped and had a little chat with their occupants. Poor they are, indeed,—with a poverty which has no parallel in happy America, and which cannot be conceived by those who have not seen it. And just now doubly and trebly poor by reason of lack of rain and famine prices of food. Yet it is just among these poor of earth that the Gospel of the kingdom of heaven has taken root most widely. Out of these Pariahs, of no caste and below caste, the Lord is raising up in India, not only a seed to serve Him, but a Christian society—not a caste—which is already beginning to command respect, and differs widely from the order out of which it springs.

CHAPTER VIII.

VELLORE TOWN, TEMPLE AND SCHOOLS.

VELLORE, February 18.

In the early morning of the 15th, we returned to Tindivanam, and in the afternoon took train for Vellore, under the kindly escort of Dr. John Scudder, who refused to let us come alone. We reached it long after nightfall—about 11 P. M. But here, too, warm hearts were waiting to receive us with a hearty greeting, which began at once, and extended itself over the next day. (I may as well say here and now, writing at a later day, when all our visits are completed, and to avoid repetition, that everywhere the same kind and keen interest was manifested, and the most cordial welcome extended to us. The memory of these scenes and of the kind words spoken can never be effaced).

Vellore, as a town, is very interesting, lying embowered in trees at the foot of three jagged hills, all of them crowned with fortifications, and having within its limits a most picturesque fort, dating, perhaps, from the end of the eleventh century. The walls are of hewn stone, many of them of large size, and fitted together with that exactness which characterizes the old masonry of India. A moat two hundred feet in width surrounds it, still filled with water. Within the fort is a temple, now desecrated and open to every one, but once sacred to Jolagandar Ishwara, "the god that dwells in water," another name for Shiva. It is entered through a pagoda, or "gopuram," of seven stories and one hundred feet in height, its sides covered to the very summit with grotesque figures. Two figures in dark-blue granite guard the entrance, of which the monolithic door-posts must be at least twenty feet in height. Passing through this gigantic doorway one enters an open court of large extent, having in its centre the holy place, with its surrounding chambers, in which the image of the god was once kept, but now deserted and empty. The inmost shrine or dwelling-place is a dark, cavernous recess, to which no light is admitted from without. Around the court are porches where worshippers from a distance were wont to spend the night, the roof supported by pillars of carved stone. In one corner, and the chief feature of interest, is the " Mandapam," or chamber of marriage ; the stone roof supported by a multitude of columns richly carved, each of a single stone. Grotesque figures of the divinity and other characters of Hindu mythology, mounted on animals equally grotesque, project from and form a part of these wonderful columns. Overhead, in the centre, is an immense lotus flower, supported by circles of parrots, hanging by their claws with heads downward, all in stone. This chamber, or hall, is said to be one of the finest in India. The drive around the fort, beside the moat, and under avenues of stately tamarind trees, is one of great beauty.

Not far removed are the tombs of the wives and family of Tippu Sultan, carefully guarded and kept in excellent preservation.

Vellore has its chief interest for us as one of the stations of our Mission and the home of the Girls' Boarding School. It has been occupied for the last twelve years by Dr. and Mrs. Jared W. Scudder, with their daughter, Miss J. C. Scudder, Mrs. Scudder having the oversight of the boarding school, and Miss Scudder of the two caste girls' schools in Arasamaram and Circar Mandy streets.

Our first visits, on the morning after our arrival, were paid to these latter schools. And what is said of these schools may be considered as applying, in the main, to all the schools of a similar character at the different stations. They have a common object—to gather into day schools, for Christian instruction especially, but with other elements as well, girls from high caste families who cannot be induced, by reason of caste, to come into the boarding school. In each station the interest in this branch of work is increasing, the number of schools is growing, and could be enlarged still further were the appropriations also enlarged. And the Secretary confesses publicly to having been so impressed with the importance of this agency that he encouraged the Mission to ask for such enlargement.

Come with us to these schools. See these bright-eyed, bright faced, smiling girls. Notice the rings and jewels and necklaces, made up sometimes of sovereigns or napoleons, and the indefinable marks of a certain high breeding which testify to the wealth and standing and importance of the families from which they come. Then hear them recite their verses of Scripture, answer questions from the catechism containing Gospel truth, and sing their lyrics in praise of that Jesus whom they are here taught to regard as their only Saviour; and remember that these are heathen girls, carrying these lessons of truth into heathen homes that in no other way could be reached by that truth. It is said, and no doubt truly, that the women of India are the staunchest supporters of its idolatry, and that many a man, who is a secret believer in Jesus, is withheld from confession by fear of the women of his household. Now surely, these girls, thus trained, can never be as ignorant or as besotted as their mothers. Nay, is it not reasonable to hope that some, even many of them, will become in heart, if not openly, the followers of Christ, and so, through their enlightenment, the way be made easier for their husbands and sons to follow and confess him? I own to being profoundly impressed with this feeling. The teaching has its effect. The truth does accomplish its mission. One of these ladies was surprised to receive from one of her girls all the family idols! On finding that she had brought them without the knowledge of her parents, she was advised to return them. This she did, at the same time saying that she could " never worship them again." The care and labor and prayer expended on these schools is well bestowed, and must have their reward.

For quite opposite reasons, a peculiar interest attaches to the Girls' Boarding School. For there the ignorant and otherwise hopeless Pariah girl is transformed, by faithful, painstaking care and the grace of God, into the intelligent Christian woman, with a kind and degree of refinement impossible otherwise, and delightful to behold. It was a beautiful surprise and welcome on Tuesday evening, when the gates of this Compound opened to us and disclosed the seventy girls of this school drawn up in lines of white, and sweetly singing. As they turned away from the verandah after being dismissed, Dr. Scudder said: "See what Christianity can do. These are all raised up out of the gutter." It seemed impossible to believe, as we assembled on Wednesday evening in the schoolroom to witness the exercises attending the distribution of prizes, which had been kindly deferred by Mrs. Scudder that we might be present. The older scholars were massed, "rank above rank," in solid mass against the wall. The room was decorated for the occasion by the girls themselves, and with invited guests was full, while many stood by the windows on the verandah. Songs and exercises, calisthenic and others, preceded the distribution. Happier faces, more lustrous eyes or beaming smiles could not be seen anywhere. No wonder that these girls are themselves coveted as prizes by the young men who leave the schools and enter the service of the Mission, nor that one of Mrs. Scudder's chief cares is to make a wise and proper distribution in this case also.

The many friends and patrons of this school and these girls, would have been interested to go with us the following day and see them at their work, and to inspect their school and bed and dining-rooms—the latter a long and wide verandah on one side of an open court. Some of the classes were studying or reading or reciting in English or Tamil. Some, budding teachers in the Normal department, were trying their 'prentice hand on groups of small urchins gathered in for them to experiment upon. The bell rang for dinner, and the long line filed out into the court; a few proceeded to the kitchen, and from thence handed out the heaped-up bowls of rice and curry, which were passed from hand to hand till each one had her portion. Then sitting down, each with her bowl before her, they waited reverently while one of their number asked God's blessing on their meal; then curiously, while that mysterious instrument, the kodak, was levelled at them; then shyly, as though they would not eat while strangers were looking on. So we turned and left them with a farewell "salaam," thoroughly in love with the Female Seminary at Vellore.

Even at the risk of making this already long letter too long altogether, mention ought to be made of the meeting this morning in the church, when the native brethren, the girls' school, and helpers and representatives from neighboring villages were present. The church, its walls and columns dressed with garlands of green, and pulpit and open space with plants of variegated foliage, was filled with as attentive and appreciative an audience as one could wish to address. Several lyrics were sung, and earnest prayers offered by the native brethren. The message delivered on behalf of the Reformed Church in America to the Reformed Church in India was founded on Jude 20-25. The hearty " Amen " from the entire congregation, which followed every prayer in this and all other gatherings of these churches, and the decorous, reverent hush and quiet for a few moments after the benediction is pronounced, might well be imitated by the Church at home.

CHAPTER IX.

AMONG THE HILLS.

Coonoor, February 22

Coonoor has been for a long series of years the only sanitarium of the Mission. The excessive heat of the plains during the hot season rendered some change necessary to the missionary families, not only for comfort, but for health. Coming, as we did, in the cooler season, and constantly reminded, "Oh, this is not hot weather; this is our winter," the change, even now, was exceedingly grateful and refreshing. What it must be later on it was possible to conceive. If "winter" has days fully equal in discomfort to the "dog-days" of a heated term in the neighborhood of New York, what must "summer" be? So, till within recent years, each family has been wont to spend three of the hottest months in each alternate year at Coonoor, where the Mission has a cottage beautifully located on a wooded knoll and bearing the euphonious name of "Wyoming."

Within a few years, however, the attractive point has shifted to Kodai Kanal, on the Pulney Hills, within the field occupied by the Madura Mission of the American Board. It has the double advantage of greater elevation (being higher by one thousand feet), with more bracing air, and of uniting, in social and Christian intercourse and fellowship, with a large number of missionaries from Madura and elsewhere. Thus, not only physical but mental and spiritual refreshment and stimulus are obtained. There, too, the Mission has a house called "Arcotia," and thither every family has liberty to repair for two months in each year. Between these two retreats, each having special attractions of its own, but only one of which could be visited for lack of time, choice was not easy. The existence of a flourishing church at the former, and the presence and earnest invitation of delegates from it at Arni, finally decided us in favor of Coonoor. Nor had we reason to regret the choice.

Lying well up on the Nilgiri Hills, at an elevation of 6,100 feet above the sea level, it is not specially easy of access. Leaving Vellore at 9.30 P. M., of the 18th, under the escort of the Rev. E. C. Scudder, Jr., a railroad ride of fourteen hours brought us to Mettupalyam. There, for the present, the railroad ends, and further progress is made in a "tonga." This is a peculiar vehicle of two wheels and two seats back to back, of the nature of a dog cart, but very strong and heavy, as the needs of the road require. From this projects a heavy tongue, or pole, to which horses are attached by an iron yoke fastened securely to the saddle. The luggage is stored beneath, before, behind and on the sides. The driver and, at the most, three passengers, take their seats, the whip is cracked and off the "tonga" starts, at a rate which it seems impossible to maintain, but which is kept up for six miles, till the base of the mountain is reached. The road is for the most part well shaded, and the air loaded with fragrance. The heat is intense.

At this point a river is crossed. The bridge was swept away by a flood many months ago, and the leisurely repairs show no signs of approaching completion. Hence, it is necessary to dismount and cross a narrow foot bridge while the luggage is carried over on the heads of men and women. Another vehicle of the same description waits on the other side, and when all is duly transferred, we take our places and are off again at the same rapid pace. The road is a specially fine one, of easy grade, ascending evenly for sixteen miles. But the pace is killing, and the faithful little beasts are changed every two miles till the town is reached. Beautiful views of the mountains open before us, or are spread at our feet as we ascend—the slopes clothed with forests of waving and graceful bamboos or straight and stately Areca palms for many miles.

The town of Coonoor lies in an amphitheatre of wooded hills, its white walls gleaming brightly against the dark and heavy masses of green. It is not specially attractive—no Indian town that we have seen is, with the exception of Vellore. But the foreign residents live in cottages and villas perched on the adjacent summits, of which there are many, and commanding magnificent views. The woods are penetrated and intersected by roads, built in the highest style of the art, kept in perfect repair, and level as a floor. Trees overarch them, banks of fragrant roses, heliotrope and lantana ablaze with glory, hedge them in. One could hardly imagine or desire a more charming retreat among the hills.

In the valleys and on the slopes are many extensive coffee and tea plantations, owned by English residents, and employing thousands of coolies. Among the latter much faithful missionary work is done, and more might be.

Under the guidance of Mr. Thomas Stanes, one of these proprietors, we visited his estate of "Glendale," and were initiated into all the processes of tea-making. The plants are set in rows, sending their roots deep into the soil, and when well grown, covering the ground with a screen of dark green leaves. By heavy pruning the plants grow thick and stocky, and after being pruned put forth tender shoots of a yellowish green. It is of these tender shoots and the leaves attached to them that the tea is made—none, of the larger and darker leaves.

When this condition is attained—called a "flush"—picking begins. By judiciously timed pruning, picking is continued throughout the year. The tender leaves are taken in baskets to the factory, and there first laid out on long stretches of bagging to wither, but not to dry. When properly withered, which is accomplished in a few hours, they are transferred to a rolling machine, and thence in shallow trays to the hot-air chamber, where they are dried by fire, the "curling" being done not by heat, but by the roller. When dried sufficiently, the tea, now redolent of its peculiar flavor, is piled in heaps to be sorted by women. Then slightly heated again, it is packed, while warm, into lead-lined chests, or leaden canisters, and hermetically sealed. It is now ready for the market, and finds a ready sale in India and in Europe, and is beginning to make its way to America. Certain special sorts, secured by selecting the tips of the shoots—called "golden tips"—bring fabulous prices. A sample was given us of a kind that, at a recent sale in London, brought £5—$25—a pound.

The Church at Coonoor seems to partake of the independent spirit which usually characterizes the dwellers on mountains. Not always manifesting it in a commendable way, it is at present in a flourishing condition. It has some valuable and energetic members, and shows an aggressive and evangelistic temper that is worthy of all praise. It is also devotedly attached to the Reformed Dutch Church. When several times, in its own interest, the project has been mooted of transferring it to the care of some other mission nearer at hand than ours, it has as often declared that it would not be transferred, that if relinquished by the Arcot Mission, it would still remain the Reformed Dutch Church of Coonoor. The "Dutch" is not in brackets, either, but an integral portion of its loved and boasted title. It was reserved for us to see, for the first time, here in the mountains of India, the Lord's Supper served after the old Dutch fashion, the communicants seated at a long table running down the aisle. A number of English friends were present at the service, who have manifested a deep interest in the welfare of the Church. It was truly a feast of love, and one long to be remembered. It may be imagined that this church would not allow itself to be outdone by those on the plain, in the heartiness and cordiality of the reception accorded to its visitors. Nor was it. The scene is not only photographed in memory, but by the camera as well.

CHAPTER X.

COONOOR TO PALMANER, AND THE THEOLOGICAL SEMINARY.

PALMANER, February 25

Facilis descensus. Easy but frightful! We started from Coonoor Tuesday morning after prayer in the church, with the school and some of the native brethren, commending one another to the grace of God. The same sort of vehicle received us, drawn by two diminutive, scrubby little ponies, that seemed each moment in danger of falling and being run over and killed. The driver plied his lash relentlessly, and on they flew, round the sharp corners and down the smooth incline. The lazy bullocks creeping up had hardly time to hear the driver's shout and crawl out of the path before we were on them, past them, down and down and down, as fast as the little feet could fly. With only one change of ponies we accomplished, in an hour and a half, the sixteen miles that had taken several hours in the ascent. The fervent ejaculation of at least one member of the party on reaching the foot of the mountain was: " No more tonga rides for me." By 1.25 P.M. we were once more on board the cars, from which we descended at 2.30 the following morning, at Gudiyatam, prepared for a long bullock ride of twenty-six miles to Palmaner.

After the long, hot, dusty railway ride, there was something peculiarly refreshing in the exchange. The pace was slow, growing slower and slower still as our bullocks were exchanged, every few miles, for other and poorer ones. But the air was cool. The stars gleamed with a peculiar brightness as we caught glimpses of them through the trees which, for many miles, overhung the road. Often we came upon bullock carts whose drivers were too sleepy, and the beasts too stupid, to turn out—bursting out of the gloom only to disappear like ships in a fog at sea. Now and again we passed through a sleeping village, or one whose inhabitants were just beginning to waken and creep forth. Like shadowy ghosts they looked, wrapped in long white clothes like winding sheets. Soon the birds began to twitter in the trees, the gray East to redden toward the dawn. It found us creeping up the Ghat, among a sea of hills. Slowly the sun climbed, but not so slow as we. His rays began to scorch—the way grew hot and weary, and we sighed for the end. Happily the end was near.

Turning aside a little from the road to view a noted banyan tree, we found spread beneath its welcome shade a simple breakfast, sent forward to refresh us by the thoughtful kindness of Mrs. Wm. Scudder. It was a spot well chosen. Above us the thick spreading canopy of leaves, shutting out the sun. About us the many stems and columns of the tree, itself grown into a grove by the sending out of its branches and the dropping and rooting of their long, cable-like tendrils—if tendrils they can be called. The area covered by this tree must have been nearly two hundred feet in diameter. In the midst of the central trunk—now partially decayed—a shrine had been set up, to which offerings were evidently made. Beneath the welcome shade, seated on the ground, we paid our attention, not to the god of the tree, but to the meal furnished, and made offerings of food to our own keen appetites. Yet one can hardly wonder that, in such a country, where superstition holds all minds in thraldom—and, most of all, the country-folk—a spirit should be supposed to reside in such a temple. Refreshed and grateful, and with ponies substituted for bullocks, we were soon driving up to the bungalow at

BUNGALOW AT PALMANER, INDIA.

Palmaner, and receiving the cordial greetings of Dr. and Mrs. Scudder. Our sympathies are with them as we remember that the road over which we came is the shortest way of reaching Palmaner.

As is, or ought to be, well-known, Palmaner is the seat of the Theological Seminary in the Arcot Mission, the latest, but not the least important of such institutions pertaining to the Reformed Church. Into the history of its establishment there is no need to enter. Of the excellence of its product we had delightful demonstration in the seven graduates licensed at Arni to preach the Gospel. It was a pleasure and privilege now to visit it, doubly grateful because the life of its honored professor had been brought up again from the borders of the grave only last year. Loved as a father by his students and heartily devoted to his work of training in mind and heart the future preachers of the Church, may he long be spared to it and them.

Providence has favored the seminary in the buildings it occupies and the grounds by which they are surrounded, admirably adapted for the purpose as they are. The property of a native Rajah, they are rented for the nominal sum of rupees, 25 a month—less than $10! The grounds include several acres. The substantial bungalow, with broad verandah, spreads widely, covering not only spacious rooms for study, lecture-room, library and recitation rooms, but dormitories for the students and homes for the native teachers or professors. An adjoining building furnishes rooms for helpers who come with their wives for special training or to pursue the regular course of instruction. Four of such helpers who have entered the present Junior Class are thus accommodated. It is proposed to have a training class for their wives also, under the care of Miss M. K. Scudder, who was transferred to this station from Madanapalle at the late meeting of the Mission. It is an excellent plan, and one that must produce good results in the villages or towns to which these helpers may hereafter be assigned.

The great, perhaps the only, lack in this situation is the want of a sufficient field for evangelistic effort on the part of the students immediately about them, or within easy reach. The village itself is small. A neat little church of white, overlooking a prettily shaded tank, accommodates the not large village congregation. Bazar and feast days and Sundays, however, afford opportunities for preaching by the students, which are faithfully embraced. And it was pleasing to note, in the address presented by the teachers and students, the expression of the conviction that "India must be brought to Christ, not by Americans but by Hindus." This is the true philosophy of evangelization for this and every other heathen country. To raise up the men to do this work on the ground, is the high purpose and the blessed office of this "school of the prophets." May there yet come forth from it, by the blessing of God, men of mental force and spiritual power, who shall be able mightily to move the hearts of their countrymen and turn multitudes to righteousness.

CHAPTER XI.

MADANAPALLE, BY WAY OF PUNGANUR.

MADANAPALLE, March 7

Our march from Palmaner to this place was begun at 6.30 A.M. of February 27. The first stage was made by coolie power, three men pulling and three pushing from behind, and at a fairly rapid pace. Thus we made seven miles to a small village, where Dr. Chamberlain's carriage, with a pair of bullocks, was found waiting for us. In this we journeyed slowly for twelve miles more, the sun sending down his scorching rays, and everything about us, as well as ourselves, testifying to their power. It was sad to note the increasing evidences of the effect of long continued drought. The region from hence northward and eastward has been the most affected by lack of rain and consequent scarcity of food, distress and famine prices. Scarcely a tank had any water. Field after field, thousands of acres in the aggregate, lay perfectly bare, no attempt having been made to cultivate them. The earth was hard and baked, as though turned to stone, and many trees were leafless. With no hope of rain for at least two months, the prospect was disheartening indeed.

Our journey of nineteen miles brought us near noon to Punganur. This is a considerable town nearly midway between Palmaner and Màdanapalle. It is the abode and capital of a Rajah who has a sort of nominal suzerainty over the district, and has shown great favor to the Mission and its work. His house in town, by courtesy as well as by contrast called "palace," is always at the service of the missionaries when staying in or passing through the town. There we were received and entertained by the Rev. and Mrs. W. I. Chamberlain and Miss M. K. Scudder, the Rajah himself being absent. A band of men with native music met and escorted us within the court, where a brass band, maintained by the prince, greeted us with somewhat discordant strains. At the entrance stood a large elephant, and within the court were cages containing tigers, leopards, monkeys, etc., for the prince's delectation and that of the public.

The High School here is known as the American Mission High School, having been placed entirely under the care of the Mission, or of the Rev. Wm. Chamberlain as representing it. Though its pupils are non-Christians, the Bible forms a prominent text-book. It is attended by two sons and two nephews of the Rajah, who pursue the same studies, and are subject to the same regulations and discipline as the other scholars. The prince bestows on it a considerable subsidy, which, together with fees and government grants, makes it more than self-sustaining. There is, also, a flourishing Caste Girls' School under the care of Miss M. K. Scudder, who comes frequently fifteen miles from Madanapalle to visit it. It is taught by a bright and interesting Hindu widow. A reading room is opened in the centre of the town and has many visitors, some of them among the officials and principal men. A good supply of periodicals and reading matter is provided, largely through the enterprise of the intelligent and indefatigable helper, Lazar Marian. All these places it was our privilege to visit and inspect.

The prize distribution in the High School had been deferred for our coming. Attended by native music and a curious crowd of followers, we repaired thither after a comforting breakfast in the palace. A heathen festival was being celebrated in a neighboring town, and had drawn away large numbers of the people. But the handsome and commodious school building was thronged, notwithstanding, with an eager company of pupils, officials and friends. The exercises were all in English, much to our relief and edification, and were understood of the majority. The attention and apparent interest never flagged, and "good points" were quickly seen and appreciated. It was interesting to listen to the report of the headmaster and the declamations by some of the scholars, who admirably performed their parts, and to see the happy faces of the favored ones as the prizes were put into their hands. And it was doubly interesting to note the respectful attention with which words insisting on the truth and value of the Bible, and the importance of its study to a true knowledge of God, were listened to by such an audience. In fact, few things have impressed me more deeply on the many occasions when such things have been uttered in the hearing of Hindus and Mohammedans alike. Does it betray a concealed conviction that, after all, the Bible is true, and God's revelation to man?

From the High School the same procession escorted us to the reading room, which was soon filled to its utmost capacity, the leading officials of the town heading and acting as spokesmen for the rest. Thence to the Girls' School, where the bright faces, delicate forms and features, and abundant jewels, with which we have become so familiar, were again presented to our vision as the happy little ones rose and gracefully saluted us with "salaams" and "Good morning." These schools are pleasing as pictures of girlish beauty and awakening thought, but far more as promises of better things in store for the women into which these girls will grow, and for others like them, through the lessons they are learning here. We could not but feel that, with such influences at work, and with the faithful preaching of the Gospel, there is much hope for Punganur.

Another fifteen miles, this time by horses, brought us to Madanapalle. It was 6.30, and the evening shades were gathering as we approached the village and the Mission compound. Here, too, as usual, the " Welcome " overflowed and met us on the way. Borne on its tide we floated within the gates, where the girls of the Boarding School, as at Vellore, were waiting to receive us with happy songs. Two little maidens, with aprons full of flower petals, scattered them in the road before us till we reached the house, where, on the broad verandah, Dr. and Mrs. Chamberlain gave us their hearty greeting, and we were at home once more. Those happy, kindly, hospitable homes in India! We can never forget them, nor the Christian affection that flowed to us in them all.

It is impossible here, as it has been elsewhere, to enter into details as I would like and the condition of things and memorable incidents deserve. Else you should hear of the daily prayers in Telugu on the verandah; the grand reception accorded us on Wednesday evening, with song and poem and addresses composed for the occasion; the Girls' Boarding School and that of the boys, both in the same compound with the home of the missionaries and under their immediate eye, and both in flourishing condition; the town schools, where more than a hundred heathen children are gathered daily for instruction; the Sunday-schools, in one of which we saw 150 of these heathen children, and heard them repeat the Catechism and texts of Scripture, and sing the praise and love of Jesus; the communion service on our second Sabbath, when the little church was thronged with reverent communicants, and words of cheer and counsel were spoken in Telugu and English; all these and more deserve fitting mention, but cannot have it here.

On Monday afternoon of each week is held the meeting of the Y. P. S. C. E. The teachers and older scholars in the Boarding School, with some of the helpers, are divided into bands which go, on every Sabbath, to the surrounding villages and preach the Gospel. On Monday they meet for prayer and counsel, and each band gives, through its leader or captain, its report of the work done the day before. It was interesting to hear them, one after another, rise and state whither they had gone, how they had fared, and how many had heard through them the words of life. One of their number, John Yesuratnam, one of the recent licentiates, waxed very earnest in his plea for these benighted villagers, and prayed that at least four missionaries might be sent from America to aid those now laboring in the Telugu field. This young man is the son of John Souri, one of the pastors of the Madanapalle church, whose name is known to many in America, more especially to the Sunday school at Kinderhook. That his earnestness was not affected I had this striking proof. When his first month's salary of eleven rupees was paid him, he returned *ten*, wishing it to be given to the work of the Lord as a kind of first-fruits. (A similar case was reported to me at Arni, of a young man who had failed to pass his examinations for a certificate, and had afterward pursued his studies with the advice and aid of the missionary. Having thus succeeded in obtaining the desired certificate, and have been taken into the employ of the Mission, he brought back his entire salary for the first month as a thank-offering for the success the Lord had granted him.) Comment is needless.

CHAPTER XII.

AMONG THE TELUGU VILLAGES.

MADANAPALLE, March 7

ONCE a year the helpers of each station are gathered at their station for examination on subjects previously assigned, and on which they are supposed to have prepared themselves by study throughout the year. The examination is in writing, and simultaneous at all the stations. Somewhat elaborate papers are drawn up, in English for those who understand that language, and for the rest in Tamil and Telugu. Judging from the English specimen I saw, one must have a pretty thorough knowledge of the books or topics embraced to be able to answer at all creditably the questions proposed. Last week this examination came off, so that we came upon it here at Madanapalle. For those who have not had the advantage of training in the Theological Seminary, as by far the larger number of the helpers have not, such an examination, and the study it involves, must be of the highest value. It serves to keep their minds employed on something beyond their round of duties, gives them an incentive to study, familiarizes them with the books of Scripture and the doctrines under review, and, altogether, tends to furnish them more thoroughly for their work. Under all the circumstances it would be hard to devise a system better adapted to secure this result.

Anxious to see something of the villages in the Telugu field, as well as in the Tamil, I accepted the Rev. Wm. Chamberlain's invitation, to accompany him to two of the remoter ones, lying near together, eighteen miles north of Madanapalle. It is among the villages that the hardest and most laborious, yet often the most successful and fruitful, work is done. At Tindivanam, for example, the village congregation is not large, nor the work, apart from the schools, exacting. But the villages connected with it embrace a number of flourishing congregations and several organized churches, and are scattered over a wide extent of country. While nominally, and only nominally, the pastor of the station church, the missionary is virtually the bishop of a spreading diocese, including all these villages and churches. It is so at Madanapalle, with this exception, that, as yet, no church has been organized outside of the town itself, and communicants in the villages look to that as their church centre and home. For this reason the church has two native pastors, the Rev. P. Souri, who has the special care of the town congregation, and the Rev. John Souri, whose special duty it is to look after the sheep scattered among the villages.

The two selected for our visit were Timmareddipalle and Nalcheruvapalle, lying opposite one another on either side of the great northern road. Starting about noon, in Dr. Chamberlain's large carriage drawn by bullocks, we made our way slowly through the drought and famine stricken region of which I have already spoken in a special note. It was after four when we arrived at Nalcheruvapalle and entered the little church. No description that I can give—no language of which I am master—can convey any impression of the reality of these villages, or of the vast majority of those one sees in travelling through this country. The irregular and narrow street or alleys, the low mud walls and thatched roofs, the half-clad people and unclad children, the miserable curs that bark and rush at every comer, the sheep and goats, cattle and fowl, sharing the earth-walled courts or yards in common with their owners, these and other features must be seen to be appreciated. Yet even in the midst of such unpromising surroundings the Lord has His own, called, chosen and faithful ones, many of whom shine as lights in a dark place. The little church of earth—used, also, for a school-room—and the helper's house, humble enough, though by contrast bright, stand side by side, a little withdrawn from the main village, on the slope and near the summit of a rocky knoll. "Up to the house of the Lord" soon came the Christian people—poor of the poorest, yet with a treasure in their hearts of which their neighbors did not know. They have sore need of it, and may it stand them in good stead in these trying times. Seated before us on the floor, with faces intent, it was a pleasure to speak to them of their far-off friends and brethren in America, and of their interest in and love for them—of the differences that separated and the essential unities that bind them all, here and there, into one body in Christ Jesus. But it was sad, afterward, to hear their story of want and privation, and their apprehensions for the future, during the long months yet to come when no rain is to be looked for. Some words of cheer and hope it was possible to speak, but they seemed empty in the presence of such real and pressing need.

After our evening meal, and in the gathering darkness, we took our way across the fields and highway to Timmareddipalle, preceded by a faithful company bearing a lantern, singing lyrics, and accompanied by a stupendous horn of brass, from which, ever and anon, proceeded ear and heaven-splitting blasts and shrieks. These served their purpose of arousing the neighboring villagers, who mustered in strong force to meet us, with lanterns and torches, and musical (?) instruments, both wind and string. It was a weird spectacle, and one not soon to be forgotten. Yet swarthy faces beamed kindly on us out of the darkness, and voices of hearty welcome sounded cheerily in our ears. This was the first village in this region to receive the Gospel, and here, after some strange and trying vicissitudes, it still retains an apparently firm hold. The little church, though larger than the other, was hardly large enough to contain the throng that gathered. Seated before us on the floor, a compact mass of black, illuminated (?) by the feeble flare of a single lantern, which twice went out and left us all in total darkness, it was yet an interesting audience to speak to. The incident of the extinguished and rekindled light made no break in the attention—it may have been a common thing—while it served as a fruitful theme for speech. It was hard to get away from these good friends, after the service was concluded, so far did they insist on going with us on our way.

At length the waiting carriage was reached—the garlands and cocoanuts and rock-candy, with which we had been gifted, as well as our weary selves, deposited therein, and then at last and finally we said farewell. By an ingenious arrangement of its owner, the seats of this carriage are capable of being so adjusted as to form a bed, a great convenience where travelling is so largely in the night. On this we stretched ourselves. The couch was easy and the road was smooth. Sleep should have come but would not, to one pair of eyes at least. It would have been, indeed, a pity to lose in slumber that strange journey under the bright and silent stars. More numerous than they were the thoughts that crowded on the mind, of the scenes through which we had just passed; of the great multitudes in this land of darkness who see no bright light before them or above them, and know nothing of the God who made the stars and them; of the faithful toilers, all too few, to whom such rewards have already been given, and larger yet shall be, please God, and of those in far-off America, in our happy land and our loved church, to whom the cry of these millions still goes out. God help them to hear and heed.

CHAPTER XIII.

CHITTOOR, KATPADI AND ARCOT.

MADRAS, March 14

AFTER Madanapalle, there remained two stations yet to be visited, Chittoor and Arcot. To accomplish these it was necessary to make a very early start from Madanapalle, which we did at 4 A. M. of the 8th in company with the Rev. W. I. Chamberlain. A ride of twelve miles, with bullocks, lay before us before reaching the railroad at Vayalpad. These early morning—and, indeed, the night—rides are far pleasanter than if made by day. The air is cool, and has a freshness which soon disappears when once the burning sun lifts his face above the horizon. The very bullocks seem to love these hours, and travel far better than in the heat of day.

Vayalpad is at present the nearest railway station to Madanapalle—far better than sixty miles, which was the shortest distance until this new line was opened. In a few weeks, however, they expect to have another several miles nearer. The town is of considerable size, and the inhabitants are still intensely bigoted. The evidences of this fact were everywhere before our eyes in the many small temples—none of them new, however—and the frequent and very peculiar shrines which abound, on small, square stone platforms, exalted on four stone pillars that must be from fifteen to twenty-five feet high. This height gives them a very singular, long-legged appearance. In spite, however, of the bigotry and the obtrusive manifestations of heathenism, a hold has been obtained, and we were glad to find and visit the interesting schools which are kept up there. A rusty car, covered with images of various divinities, and mounted on heavy solid wheels of wood bound with iron, and in a most decayed condition, stood by the wayside. Its condition seemed to indicate the approaching decay of the superstitions which gave it its existence, and which still prompt its use at certain seasons, when it is drawn through the town amid the acclamations of multitudes.

Chittoor is an unusually attractive town, as towns in India go. Its streets are broader, many of them well shaded with noble trees of various kinds, and its houses and shops seemed of a rather better character. It is a place, too, of considerable importance, both the Collector and the Judge of the district having here their homes and their official residence as well. As regards the Mission, too, it is an important centre, or at least has been, and should be again. A good mission bungalow, in good condition, awaits the occupancy of a missionary, whose coming should not long be delayed. In the same large compound, beside the houses of the Catechist, Jacob Raji and the teachers, are the fine buildings formerly occupied by the Girls' School—the "Arcot Female Seminary,"—and, after that was removed to Vellore, by the Arcot Academy. All these buildings are ready for use, and it gave me a feeling of sadness to walk through the deserted rooms. Chittoor, also, has the finest church building in the Mission, erected under the direction of Dr. Wm. Scudder many years ago. There, after visiting the schools, it was a pleasure to meet a large congregation, representing not only the town itself, but several of the outlying villages, to receive their address of greeting and their fragrant garlands and copious sprinkling of rose water, and respond in such terms as one could command. Their review of the work that had been done there, and their grateful mention of the names of the several missionaries who had occupied the station in former years, did but intensify the wish to be able to assure them that the Church in America would readily increase the number of its missionaries to supply their want and that of other stations. "The harvest" here and in other places yet to be mentioned, might truly be great if the laborers were not so few.

From Chittoor to Katpadi is a short run by rail. Having enjoyed the kind hospitality of Mrs. Sewell, who is herself the daughter of an honored missionary, the late Dr. Hay, and who, with Judge Sewell, her husband, manifests in many ways her interest in and sympathy with the people and the work of the Mission, we left Chittoor by a late evening train for the latter place. Here one of the oldest and ablest of the pastors is stationed, the Rev. Abraham William.* Tall and slender in form, with a bright eye and keenly intelligent countenance, he might easily, but for the dark shade of his skin, pass for a typical Yankee. Here he has been helped of God to build up a flourishing church, and to secure a very neat and attractive church building. In this new church it was his strong desire that we should hold a service. And it was to fulfil a conditional promise to that effect that we were now on our way. Few interior towns, or even cities, in India have hotels or inns for the entertainment of travelers. To meet their necessities, simple houses of shelter, called "dak bungalows," are maintained at government expense. A butler or steward is in charge, on whom the traveller may make his requisitions for food, etc., and to whom a small charge is paid for the accommodation afforded. Not all are equally good or comfortable. Since the establishment of railways some have been discontinued altogether, and are falling

---

* It is sad to be obliged to record the death, since the above was written, of this able, intelligent and devoted servant of God. He rests from abundant and fruitful labors, and his works follow him.

into decay. To such a refuge we were conducted, with flaming torch and lanterns, by our friends. We found this cheerfully lighted, a table spread with tea, etc., a bedstead and two or three chairs, and passed a very comfortable night.

The little church is directly opposite the bungalow, and service had been arranged for six o'clock the next morning. In the bright moonlight the arch and other external decorations provided for the unusual event were plainly to be seen. Long before daylight it was necessary to be stirring, and while eating our simple breakfast within the open door, we could see the people streaming through the opposite gate. Taking our way over at the hour appointed, under the conduct of Pastor Abraham, we found the church already filled. The programme arranged included the baptism, by the Secretary, of five infants, over whom, after the service had been read in Telugu by Brother Chamberlain, it was a pleasure to administer the rite which admitted them, visibly, at least, into the fold of Christ. A number of East Indians, or Eurasians, of mixed blood, helped compose the congregation. Some of them, we were glad to hear, are active and helpful in the Church. The address, in English, was composed and written, I believe, by one of them, and was accompanied as usual with garlands and other tokens of regard. On leaving the church, we found the village school drawn up in parallel lines just outside the gate for our inspection—bright, restless little fellows, many of them, but answering well the questions asked, and evidently heartily enjoying the novel occasion. A call at Pastor Abraham's house, and also at another which he is building, where prayer was offered at his request, concluded our visit. It was an "object lesson" of the way in which the Church of Christ must chiefly grow in this and other heathen lands, through the care and labors of faithful men raised up and called of God from among the people themselves. From a street boy to a successful pastor, from a cattle-driver to a faithful preacher of the Word and leader of men—these and other such are the terms that characterize the extremes, the beginning and the present of these men. And many a most interesting story lies between, some of which I would be glad to relate if there were time and space. To me they are among the most conspicuous and blessed fruits of the Mission's work, and on them and those who shall be associated with or come after them, largely rests, under God, the hope of the Church in these dark lands.

The early service in Katpadi was made necessary by an early departure, at 7.20 A. M., for Arcot, the last station to be visited, but by no means the least important. Here is the hospital, so long under the care of different members of the Mission, and now in the charge of the Rev. L. R. Scudder, M. D., and also the Arcot Academy, now the Arcot Mission High School, in charge of Mr. H. J. Scudder. It is also the centre of a large and prosperous village work. It was a pity to have only two days to spend at this station, but this was all the time allowed by other and important engagements. It was, therefore, very full.

The hospital and high school, as well as the Mission bungalow in which Dr. Scudder lives, are located, not in the town of Arcot, which lies two miles beyond, but at Ranipet, between the town and station, and three miles from the latter. Met at the station by both the brethren named, we were escorted into the village by a goodly company, who had come out about a mile to receive us with music and banners. After resting a few moments, and dismissing our escort, we visited the hospital. The commodious buildings, affording accommodation for the various wards and offices, are provided by government, which also furnishes the appropriations necessary for its maintenance. Though thus, and to this degree, a government institution, it is also, and quite distinctly, a missionary agency, for which the Church furnishes nothing but the supervising missionary and responsible head. Religious instruction is given daily to all the patients, and the truths there communicated are carried by them to points far removed and widely separated. But the care of such an institution makes large demands upon the time and strength of the missionary in charge. With the other work of the station necessarily devolving upon him, he is cut off from doing medical work in the villages, which he feels has promise of far greater and better results. Nor can he do for the women, who are often in far greater need of help than men, what a physician of their own sex could do. For all these reasons Dr. Scudder urges that such a physician be sent out to his assistance. I cannot doubt that his plea is justified by the circumstances, and that to grant it would be eminently wise.

The Arcot Mission High School is beautifully located on lands and in buildings also furnished by the government, free of cost except for repairs and maintenance. The buildings were formerly occupied by cavalry when a considerable military force was maintained here. That force has long been withdrawn—as also from Vellore and Arni—and left many substantial buildings behind it without use or occupancy. On a gentle eminence just out of the village, and overlooking a landscape of unusual breadth and beauty, closed in by mountains, with a broad, open lawn sloping away from it toward the town, stands the modest bungalow occupied by the principal. In the rear of it is a long row of buildings, devoted to the school, comprising storerooms, dormitories and recitation rooms, and a smaller building for library and reading-room. The buildings are substantial, roomy and attractive, and the accommodation sufficient for even a much larger number of pupils than are now in attendance. As we appeared upon the campus some of the larger scholars were undergoing military drill, followed by gymnastic exercises, which they executed with great precision and agility under the direction of a trained master. At the tap of the bell the ground was deserted, and all repaired to the large hall, where were gathered not only the entire school, but also the helpers and members of the church and congregation. The spacious room was filled for the reception of the guests of the day, and the presentation of addresses. A similar gathering filled it at a later hour in the evening, when another address was presented by the day scholars, expressing their gratitude for being admitted to the privileges of the school. These are non-Christian young men from the town, and their admission is a new thing in this school. Much good is hoped for from it, both to the young men and to the school itself. In order to signalize the occasion, there followed the presentation by the boys of a sacred drama, composed, I believe, by one of the teachers, and founded on the history of Daniel and Darius. The king and his attendants were arrayed in gorgeous bravery, the prophet in conspicuous meekness. The boys entered into the scene with spirit, and the exhibition lasted till a late hour of the night.

The church, next morning, was the scene of a very interesting service, which began at the early hour of 7.15. It was the baptism of a man with his entire family, six souls in all, who had for twenty years been at heart a Christian, and had at length come to the point of open confession of the Lord Jesus Christ. His wife, who had not shared his faith at first, had come to a knowledge of the Saviour. Other hindrances had been removed, and now, acknowledging the error of his long delay, he desired to be numbered among the people of God. Two of his sons were scholars in the High School. It was a privilege to administer to them the rite of baptism, and commend them to God and the Word of His grace, and also to address to the assembled church some brief words of counsel and encouragement as from the Church in America.

CHAPTER XIV.

OLD ARCOT AND THE GUDIYATAM CONFERENCE.

MADRAS, March 14

A DRIVE of two miles to the old town of Arcot was next in order. The road lay across the broad bed of a river now entirely dry, but in the rainy season often a raging stream. The hot sun beat down upon the scorching sand, in which the wheels so buried themselves that progress would have been well nigh impossible if four or five coolies had not assisted the struggling pony by pulling or pushing from behind. A fine stone causeway is in process of construction across the river bed, which will greatly relieve this difficulty, affording a fine, smooth road. Arcot was once a strongly fortified city, and remains of the old fortifications are still standing. Other remains lie in confusion where they were thrown when the walls were blown up many years ago—immense masses of brick masonry, solid and indestructible as rocks, even in their ruins. One gate, called "Clive's Gate," remains intact, with "Clive's Chamber" surmounting it. The history of the city is inseparably connected with the fame of that great leader who, from a civilian clerk became one of England's most skillful generals, and here won one of his earliest and most signal victories—with a small force capturing the city against fearful odds and maintaining possession against odds still greater. Once the seat of powerful Mohammedan princes, it retains nothing of what splendor it may formerly have possessed. The palace is an utter ruin, hardly a vestige remaining to mark the site where it once stood, and the whole town wears a look of decay.

But Mohammedanism of the most bigoted type is still strong in it, as the numerous mosques and the intense spirit of opposition to the Gospel abundantly testify. For this reason it has been extremely difficult to get and hold a footing there. This is now held by a school which we visited, our presence being the signal for the gathering of numbers of the people. They looked on while the simple exercises were gone through, and heard some plain declarations of Gospel truth from the lips of the children. Out of the mouths of these "babes" it may be that the Lord will yet perfect praise in this stronghold of the false prophet.

The town of Wallajah, two miles from Ranipet in another direction, is altogether the neatest and most attractive I have seen in India. Its people were once quite wealthy, but the location of the railroad and its station at a few miles' distance has destroyed much of its prosperity, as has so often happened in other lands. The road thither is shaded by rows of trees on either side. The streets are broad, measurably clean, with many trees, and lined by houses well built and white. The whole effect is one of neatness, cleanliness and comfort quite unusual in an Indian village, so far as I have seen. The work here is represented by two schools, one for boys and one for girls, which, after being visited singly, came together in the more spacious building occupied by the boys, for our reception. A reading-room is also maintained on the principal street. But the best influence in Wallajah, and the most hopeful fact, is the new preacher and helper stationed there; the best scholar, by all confession, of the recently graduated class from the theological seminary, and one of those licensed by the Classis at Arni. Of good caste, and having connections in town, and being himself a young man of ability, earnest spirit and piety, there is good reason to hope that he may be able to win his way in spite of the opposition which has here been very bitter and persistent.

It is an unfortunate necessity—yet a necessity it seems—that the Mission should be compelled to employ as teachers, in some departments, men who are not Christians. They can get no others competent to do the work, while the religious instruction is confided to Christian teachers. Some of these men are, no doubt, Christians at heart—that is to say intellectually convinced of the falsehood of idolatry and the truth of Christianity. It may be that some, if not all of them, will yet be found openly on the side of Christ. Certainly, some whom I have heard, do not hesitate to speak quite boldly the thing they really think. A most singular instance of the kind we met at Wallajah, the second master in the girls' school. He showed us special attention, following us to the reading-room, and in various ways manifesting his interest in the work. Of him we were told that he does not hesitate to advise others to become Christians. In one instance he pleaded for more than hour with the mother of our young helper, Thavamoni, urging her by every consideration to renounce heathenism and accept Christianity. Such men, and there are doubtless many like them, are in a hopeful yet critical state. They need, and they should have the prayers of Christians that they may come to the full and personal knowledge and acceptance of the truth as it is in Jesus.

We could not leave Arcot, or Ranipet, without paying a visit to the little cemetery. For there lies buried all that is mortal of our good brother Hekhuis, side by side with the infant daughter of Mr. and Mrs. Conklin. It was a gloomy place save for that little spot, kept bright and green, with flower and plant, with daily watering and faithful care. He sleeps among the people he lived to bless, and his memory lives fresh as the plants that grow beside his grave. "Dead on the field of battle," he seemed certainly not less worthy of memorial and monument than the British officers by whose tombs he lies surrounded.

It had for some time been the desire of the Mission to hold a General Conference of all the missionaries and as many of the helpers as could be gotten together, for the increase of spiritual life and power and the discussion of practical topics relating to mission work. It was hoped that by thus gathering for mutual counsel and united prayer the helpers might be encouraged and stimulated, a new baptism of the Spirit sought and obtained, and a healthful impulse given to the work. This Conference it had been determined to hold at Gudiyatam on Friday, Saturday and Sunday, March 11–13. Gudiyatam is a large town of Hindus and Mohammedans, about twenty miles from Katpadi and eighty or ninety from Madras. The Mission has long desired to occupy it as a permanent station, and twenty years ago assigned it to Dr. John Scudder as his field and residence. But the Board was not then ready to furnish the means necessary to provide a house, and it remains unoccupied to-day. I was glad of the opportunity to see something of the town myself, and of its importance as a station. As the 10th had come and nearly gone, it was necessary to take our way thither. With Dr. Lewis and Mr. Henry Scudder we took the evening train, and were joined at Katpadi by others of the Mission and a goodly number of helpers.

A fine grove of mango trees, three miles from the station and lying just outside the town, had been obtained. Thither we repaired in "jutkas," which, in bewildering number and indescribable uproar and confusion, met us at the gate. The "jutka" is a little two-wheeled cart, of long, narrow body, and covered with a rounding roof of palmleaf matting. Within it one can either sit or stretch himself out at length upon the floor. With a mattrass and pillow, and the springs with which the vehicle is furnished, quite a comfortable bed can be made and sleep obtained, and many a missionary journey is thus made, both by day and night. The driver sits upon the shaft, and the lively little pony, stimulated by voice and lash, rushes over the road at quite a rapid pace. The motion is not altogether agreeable at first, and one is apt to be knocked about rather unceremoniously. But a little experience and judicious adjustment of person and "personal effects" soon enable him to ride quite comfortably and even to enjoy it.

The road for three miles lay in bright moonlight, shadowed by rows of trees which lined it on either side. The grove, when reached—as also on the morrow and in the broad light of day—presented a scene of perfect beauty. A multitude of noble mangoes—the largest I have seen—with immense trunks and wide-spreading branches, and at convenient distance for pitching the largest tents while shading them all completely from the sun—formed an ideal place for such a gathering—truly one of "God's first temples." Broad, square platforms with ascending steps on each side had been prepared by collectors and other officials, who make this their camping-ground when visiting this portion of their district. Several tents belonging to members of the Mission were already pitched when we arrived, in which, with small reluctance or delay, we slept that night in peace. Early next morning two large tents arrived, kindly loaned for the purpose, and sent over from Chittoor by Judge Sewell, of whom I have spoken, and Mr. Le Fanu, the collector of the district, who often and in many ways has manifested his interest in the Mission and his desire to aid it. These were so pitched as to form a pavilion, in which the exercises of the Conference were held, the one raised a little above the other, making a covered platform, and the other, with outspread wings, forming the audience chamber. Over all the trees spread their glorious roof of green, their trunks forming massive pillars in broad aisles on every hand.

The exercises began at 1 P. M. of Friday the 11th. All the missionaries were present but Dr. Jared Scudder, who was detained by illness in his family, but arrived later in the day, and Dr. Chamberlain, who for his health, was on the way to Darjeeling. Of helpers and theological students there were 120. The presence of so large a number, in view of the fact that their coming was purely voluntary and chiefly at their own expense, was a cheering evidence of their interest in the objects of the Conference. The sight of them from the platform, seated in compact mass on the pavilion floor, their earnest countenances turned toward the speakers, was inspiring. And when their turn came to join in the discussions, it was refreshing to see the readiness with which they rose and delivered themselves of brief and earnest addresses, or led in fervent prayers. One utterly ignorant of the language could not but feel how heartily they entered into the spirit of the occasion. It fell to my lot to make the opening address on the assigned topic, the "Means of Obtaining Power From On High." I count it a great privilege to have been permitted to do it, though hampered and even oppressed by the utter impossibility of speaking directly to them in their own language. I am rejoiced to know, by a note from Dr. Jared Scudder, that the power sought seems in blessed measure to have been obtained. "Never before," he writes, "have I witnessed such a scene, either at home or here. The Spirit of the Lord came upon us with power. Missionaries, native pastors and assistants, one and all, weeping tears of joy, consecrated themselves anew to the Lord and to His service." Compelled to leave the place on the early morning of Saturday, it was not my privilege to witness these closing scenes. But I thanked God for them, as those will who read of them at home. The more abundant and mighty manifestation of the Spirit in mission fields, and, since I have been here, in this field, seems to me the thing of all others most to be desired. For this the Church at home should continually pray.

CHAPTER XV.

SILENT PREACHERS.

MADRAS, March 14

The Church has two missionaries in India of which, perhaps, it takes little account. They cannot speak or write letters, but they do excellent service none the less. They are the bicycle and the magic lantern. The former, over the admirable roads so largely found in India, makes frequent short tours, and even long ones, rapid and easy, and is much used by the younger missionaries. It attracts the wondering gaze of the people—some of whom connect it in thought and speech with the devil—and has even been used as a means of gathering a crowd to listen to the preaching of the Gospel. Of the other, the magic lantern, I had not made practical acquaintance, though I had heard much, till our last Sunday evening in Madanapalle. Then, in a broad street of the town, the pictures thrown on a screen supported against the trunk of a great tree, we witnessed its performance under the direction of the Rev. Wm. Chamberlain. The large crowd gathered seemed intensely interested as one view after another was displayed. At first, secular and even comic views were used, to win and rivet their attention. Thus caught and interested, they listened quietly to the explanation of Scripture scenes and the enforcement of lessons drawn from them by the missionary and a chosen band of earnest and effective speakers. As many as half-a-dozen forceful little sermons were thus preached in a single evening.

Large use was made of this silent teacher at Gudiyatum. On the afternoon of Friday a few of the missionaries and a large band of native helpers marched through the streets of the town, selecting places for exhibitions and inviting the people to come and see them in the evening. There were three lanterns present and at evening three bands were formed under the leadership of Dr. Lewis and the Rev. E. C. Scudder and the Rev. W. I. Chamberlain, and composed of speakers capable of addressing the crowds they hoped to gather. Each band proceeded to the place assigned, the lanterns were set up, and the pictures exhibited to crowds of people of all sorts and sizes. Giving time for the preliminaries, I followed them to town in company with the Rev. Dr. Phillips, once a missionary in Northern India, but now the Agent of the Sunday-school Union. Our jutka driver proved either stupid or malicious, or both, and we came near spending the night in driving about the streets without finding the object of our quest. At length we came upon the Rev. Wm. Chamberlain, to whom, perhaps, two hundred people had gathered, and were quietly viewing the pictures and listening to the earnest words addressed to them. Farther on we found Dr. Lewis Scudder in the midst of somewhat larger numbers. Later in the evening a disturbance arose at this place, just at the close of the exhibition and preaching. Either through mischief or in malice, an alarm of fire was raised, and the crowd stampeded. Lantern and views were overthrown, and the doctor himself narrowly escaped being roughly handled. Leaving him before any sign of disturbance had shown itself, we found the Rev. E. C. Scudder and the largest company of all in quite another part of the town. His pictures were cast upon the white wall of a house. Just around the lantern large numbers were seated on the ground, and encircling them, many deep, still larger numbers were standing. Many of the people were Mohammedans, and Dr.

Phillips spoke to them in Hindustani, asking and answering questions. Two things impressed me in connection with this method of making known the Gospel. First the admirable adaptness for reaching masses of people in a simple and yet effective manner. Two senses are appealed to, and what is caught by the eye is impressed by the voice of the living preacher on the ear. And, as a rule, the speakers seemed thoroughly alive to the nature of the opportunity, and made their addresses brief, earnest and impressive. Perhaps the brethren engaged would not care to have me say it, and perhaps, also, the feeling was due to my own inexperience. But I was deeply impressed, also, with the quiet courage—not to say heroism—required for such service, in the midst of a great city filled with a bigoted populace, and in the presence of crowds of Hindus and Mohammedans, whose apparent interest might easily be changed into the frantic fury of a mob by the fanatical appeal of some hotheaded leader. I deeply regretted not being able to remain to the close of this delightful Conference. But steamers do not wait the convenience of travellers, and having already deferred leaving India for a fortnight beyond the time assigned, I could delay no longer. Yet what I had seen, and the mingling with those brethren there, formed a most fitting and delightful close to the Arcot Mission, fraught as it was throughout with pleasure unalloyed. Bidding all farewell soon after midnight, in the solemn stillness of the grove, I took my way early on Saturday morning to Madras. We leave here to-morrow morning for Madura and Ceylon.

I have said nothing of Madras for the simple reason that I have little or nothing to say. As a city there is little about it that is attractive. It lies sprawling along the eastern shore of the Indian peninsula for a distance of several miles, without a harbor until very recently, and one wonders how a large city and port of entry, the capital of the large Presidency of that name, ever came to be planted there. Of recent years the government has caused two long breakwaters or jetties to be constructed, running out into the sea perpendicular to the shore, but curving inward near their outer extremities, thus forming a moderate sized port. Vessels can now come within it and discharge their cargo and passengers at a pier, though many still lie off in the roadstead and send them in through the surf as aforetime. Along the beach is a fine drive, where the life of the city gathers in the cool of the evening. A fine military band discourses excellent music. The roadway is thronged with vehicles of every description, from the most elegant landau or victoria to the humblest gharry. Their occupants sit and listen to the music or look off upon the sea, inhaling the refreshing breeze after the stifling day, or dismount and circle about, chatting with acquaintances or friends. It is like an immensely long ballroom, al fresco, save for the vehicles which lumber up the way.

I spoke of the town as "sprawling." Such it literally is—its various quarters being separated by almost interminable distances, with gardens or long stretches of open ground between. It has some fine buildings and some noble institutions. The Christian College of the Scotch Free Church is here, a flourishing institution with hundreds of students, beside the Presidency College, whose buildings suggest an architect's nightmare, and a native University founded by the liberality of a wealthy native resident. A vast amount of missionary work, also, has its centre here, and a fair proportion of the population is said to be under its influence. There are many fine residences with grounds or compounds about them, which give to many of the streets a straggling and suburban appearance, while some of the native quarters, notably that to the North, surpass in wretchedness and squalor anything I have seen elsewhere. Here, too, appears, in horrible frequency, that terrible deformity of disease—elephantiasis. It was no uncommon sight to see men shuffling along the street with one leg so swollen that the toes of the foot were nearly lost in the limb—resembling nothing so much as the leg of the animal from which the disease takes its name. The only relieving consideration is that it is comparatively painless to the sufferer, however painful to the beholder. In short, the whole effect of Madras upon the transient visitor is not pleasing, nor, I believe, are its attractions much greater for the permanent resident. As a city it is by no means to be compared with Bombay.

The one bright spot which relieved the impression of our stay in Madras, was the meeting with Mary Rajanayakam and the Rev. and Mrs. E. C. Scudder, Jr. The latter friends facilitated much some of the objects of our stay, and kindly saw us off for Madura and parts beyond. Mr. Scudder brought cheering tidings of the successful issue of the Conference at Gudiyatam, of which I wrote in my last letter. The former is the young medical student whom the ladies of the Particular Synod of Albany are supporting during her period of study. They have reason to rejoice in their ward, and in the choice made for them by Dr. Chamberlain. Of sweet face and winning manner, the story of her inward conflicts and the triumph of simple faith to which she had attained proved the genuine and gracious work of the Spirit within. She seemed altogether one of the sweetest women and loveliest Christians one could wish to see. If the life-work, from which she first shrank, but to which she now looks forward with consecrated hope, is carried on in the same spirit in which she pursues her studies, she cannot fail to be greatly useful.

CHAPTER XVI.

MADURA TEMPLES AND MISSION.

COLOMBO, CEYLON, March 21

For thorough discomfort and studied neglect of the convenience of travellers, commend me to the South India Railway. Having a monopoly of the traffic, it treats passengers as it pleases, and its pleasure certainly does not conduce to theirs. Travelling in India at the best, especially in the hot season, is full of discomfort. The many conveniences known to American railroads are utterly unknown here. The heat in the daytime is intense, and no provision but the hardest kind of seats is made for the night—no beds, no pillows; water, but no soap or towels. One must take all these with him or go without. A journey of 22 consecutive hours under these circumstances does not tend to make one feel happy, or specially benevolent toward those who have reduced him to such misery. Still, we were brought with safety, and that is much, from Madras to Madura, leaving the former at 7.05 A. M. of Tuesday, and arriving at Madura at 5.20 A. M. of Wednesday.

Madura is doubly interesting as one of the chief centres of heathenism in South India, if not the very chief —and also of a long established and successful Mission of the A. B. C. F. M. In the early morning of Wednesday, the 16th, we were cordially welcomed on alighting from the cars, by the Rev. J. S. Chandler, of that Mission, and escorted to his hospitable home. Under his kindly conduct we were able to see much of the city in both these aspects. The relations of this Mission and our own have always been of the happiest character, and

HEATHEN TEMPLE, MADURA INDIA.

are now still closer than before. To them, we, years ago, gave Miss Mandeville, who became Mrs. Noyes, and is still on the field with her husband ; a favor they now reciprocate by giving us Miss Gertrude Chandler, to become Mrs. Wyckoff. Their summers too are spent in company, in the delightful and healthful retreat of Kodai Kanal, on the Pulney Hills, to which the Madura Mission have long resorted, and where now, through their kindness, the Arcot Mission has a comfortable house erected under the supervision of Dr. Chamberlain, and called "Arcotia." It was one of my chief regrets in leaving India, not to be able to visit it. There can be no question that the possession and use of such Sanitariums tend to preserve the life and health of our missionaries, and prolong the terms for which they are able to remain upon the field. One needs experience in order to realize the tremendous drain upon the strength—and on the spirits also—made by the extreme, unrelenting and long continued heat to which they are subjected. Even in the cooler months, of which March may, perhaps, be considered one, it is hard to bear. Our constant thought and frequent exclamation was : "What must it be in summer !"

On such a hot day we made the tour of Madura. The great temple is an imposing monument of the superstitious idolatry that has so long ruled in this idolatrous land. It is built round a large, square tank, with four large gopurams or towers, and a number of smaller ones and numerous colonnades and passages. The gopurams are of peculiar construction, on an oblong base—the longer side facing the tank—and rising story upon story to a great height, and gradually diminishing in size as they ascend. Each story is pierced with openings and faced with images of gods and goddesses and other figures, either of wrought stone or plaster, till the entire surface seems encrusted with sculpture. The walls of the colonnades or porticos surrounding the tank, are covered with pictures in gaudy colors, apparently illustrative of Hindu mythology. As we passed through one of them a young Brahmin was intoning to a small company an explanation of some of these pictures, to which he continually pointed. The approaches to the sacred courts with roofs supported on pillars of stone, many of them highly carved, were filled with a noisy, filthy crowd of vendors and beggars, suggesting the propriety of such a purging as our Lord administered to the temple in Jerusalem. The most notable feature of the temple is the Hall of a Thousand Columns (985 exactly, I believe), which is really stupendous in size and wonderful in construction. Each column is a monolith, of varying shape, but all carved in strange and grotesque figures, armed warriors, rampant horses and lions, gods and goddesses hideous and innumerable. Though much greater in number and size, the carving and figures did not seem to me to equal those in the temple at Vellore. The inmost recesses, or sanctuaries of the god and goddess to whom, in equal proportions, this temple is consecrated, were not open to our view. They are dark chambers of solid masonry, into which no ray of light is permitted to enter, and no foot of any but the priests to intrude. But low in the wall a little orifice permits the oil, milk and melted butter poured upon the idol within to issue in a sluggish, dirty, repulsive stream. The dipping of the finger into this nauseous fluid and tasting it, purges from all sin! Still more repulsive, if possible, was the image of the sacred bull, of stone, and seated in a tank of stone—like a large bath-tub—the image black and greasy with the oil poured over it and its head crowned with flowers. The bottom of the tank was foul with the black and reeking oil that trickled down the sides of the image. It was enough to make one sick

—most of all sick at heart for the millions to whom this repulsive object was a sacred thing and this oil endowed with saving power. Its filthiness was a fit symbol of the moral pollution which characterizes Hinduism as it exists to-day, and which must forever prevent the purification and uplifting of those who still retain their faith in it.

Strongly contrasting with this temple, in outward appearance, is the Teppa Kulam, or tank temple, just outside the city. In the midst of a square tank, one mile in circuit and surrounded by a finely constructed wall of cut stone, stands a white temple literally embowered in trees of luxuriant growth, on a square island rising from the centre of the tank. Seen from the outside it is indeed a thing of beauty, though it was impossible to forget that it covered, within, objects and sights similar to those which had awakened our mingled compassion and disgust. One is oppressed by the thought of the millions on whom this system has its hold, and the strength of the hold it has upon them. In moving through the streets we passed two sacred cars, dingy with age and exposure, which workmen were busily putting into a state of repair. In a few weeks a sacred festival begins, when these streets will be thronged with hundreds of thousands of worshippers from all parts of India, and these cars will be drawn slowly through them in honor of the gods whose images they bear.

A minor festival in actual progress at the time of our visit, in a village a few miles out of Madura, and at a sacred shrine peculiarly regarded in this region, gave us an inkling of what such a gathering might be. All day long the people streamed along the road, on foot, in vehicles of every sort, singing, shouting, filling the air with uproar and with the dust raised by passing feet. It seemed as though the town and all the neighboring villages must be depopulated and the whole immense mass poured upon the village where the temple stands. The tide continued far into the night, and made it difficult to make our way into the town against the current. The next morning, we passed, on the railway, through the village where the festival was to be held that day. Long before we reached it we came upon the camps of those who had spent the night sleeping on the ground. Their number increased as we advanced, till the face of the ground seemed covered with them. There they would spend the day in celebrating the marriage of a son of the goddess who presides over half of the great temple at Madura, and then return wearied to their homes, but with no thought of the folly of the scenes and ceremonies in which they had been engaged.

It is a relief to turn away from these impressive and oppressive manifestations of the power and degradation of heathenism to the work of the Mission, which shines as a light in this dark place. Madura is the centre of a large and successful work extended over a wide field. It is, I believe, one of the oldest stations of the American Board. The methods employed differ essentially so little from those in use in our own Arcot Mission, that there is no need to enter into particulars in regard to them, though we visited with interest and pleasure the schools and churches in the city. One delightful afternoon was spent in a visit to the large school at Pasumalai (pronounced Pussumully), where more than two hundred boys and young men are under instruction in all grades, up to and including the Theological School. A few miles out of the city and on the slope of a hill, its fine white building presents quite an imposing appearance. Here are being trained for service the men who are to do "for Christ and India," in this part of the great field, what the men trained in our own High School and Theological Seminary are to do in the Arcot field. No branch of missionary labor is more important, more vitally essential than this. We were shown through the buildings by Dr. Washburn, who also told us many interesting stories of some of the young men, and the circumstances under which they had been brought into the school. Nothing could have been more kind than the reception we met with from all the brethren here, and we shall always remember them with gratitude, and our brief two days' stay with unalloyed satisfaction.

From Madura to Tuticorin we came by rail, about 100 miles, to take the steamer for Ceylon. We started in the early morning at 5.30, and the air was cool and pleasant. But the sun had no sooner risen with its fervent heat than discomfort began. We were thoroughly convinced that it was "time to get out of India." The country through which we passed lay, a great flat plain, beneath the scorching sun, low hills showing their dim outline in the distance. A dreamy haze hung over it and them. It would have reminded us of our own "Indian summer," but for the heat. This Indian summer was of a different sort. The vegetation changed its character. We saw comparatively little rice, the great staple further north, but ran through miles and miles of cotton. The plants from the car windows, looked small and shrivelled by the heat, though probably of normal size, notwithstanding. When, at length, the slow moving train drew up to the station, we seemed to have been discharged into a furnace heated seven times. The hot sun beat down on walls and streets of white, and the reflected glare seemed intolerable.

Tuticorin is a port-of-call for steamers running up and down the coast and crossing to Ceylon, the distance to Colombo being only 150 miles. Like Madras, it is a port without a harbor, and vessels lie in the roadstead at a distance of from five to seven miles. A large traffic in coolies is maintained with Ceylon, where labor is much needed on the tea plantations, and hundreds are constantly transported, by almost every steamer, either on their way over seeking work or returning with their hardly earned gains. The wages they receive are much better than in India, and their labor is more satisfactory to the planters than that of the natives of the island. A small steamer plies back and forth two or three times a week, usually carrying a full complement. The steamer we proposed to take was larger, of the British India line, and to leave on Friday, the day of our arrival, which we had timed to meet her. Unfortunately there were no signs of her coming, nor did she appear till the following day. We were thus unwillingly compelled to spend here thirty weary hours, in a place utterly devoid of interest and with no hotel worthy of the name. One there was—the only one—boasting the high-sounding title of "Royal," but it was a very decayed, decrepit and crumbling sort of royalty indeed. Discomfort was written on the outside and had taken up its abode within. Nothing redeemed it but the glorious breeze from off the sea which it directly faced, and the verandah from which we enjoyed it. Nothing could mar the beauty of the sea as it lay lapping the shore at our very feet, the sound of its gently breaking waves in our ears and the cool breeze fanning our faces. They made the heat and the long waiting tolerable.

In the early morning of Saturday our steamer, the "Scindia," appeared in the offing, and word was sent us to be ready at two o'clock to take the launch which should carry us and our belongings seven miles out to join her. At four we were all on board, and at half-past five were slowly steaming on our way and bidding a last farewell to India. It is impossible to take leave of it in these letters without making heartfelt mention of the warm kindness and affection shown us by our missionaries, the enthusiastic welcomes we everywhere received from the native brethren and churches, and the deep and lasting impressions made on our minds in regard to the great work in India in which we are engaged. What these impressions were I shall hope to have opportunity to tell more fully in other times and places.

Our short trip across the channel was saddened by the death and burial of a fellow passenger, a fine English gentleman whom we had met at Madura. With his daughter he had been making an extended tour of missions in India, intending, on his return, to spend much time in speaking of them among the Baptist churches, of which denomination he was a member. We found him ill at Tuticorin, "touched by the sun," as we were told. To move him seemed a crazy thing. But he was carried out in the launch, and hoisted on board over the ship's side, in a chair rigged for the occasion, all in the broiling afternoon sun. He soon began to fail, and though every effort was made to save him, died before midnight. At half-past ten the next morning the engine was stopped, the officers and crew and the little company of passengers gathered round the coffin hastily prepared, and the English burial service was read by your correspondent. Then, in solemn silence, all heads uncovered, the coffin was lifted and slid into the sea, there to remain till the sea shall give up its dead. His heart-broken daughter received the full sympathy of all and the loving ministrations of members of our party. The shadow of the sad event, not easy to shake off, rested on all our hearts.

We were not sorry when the shore, even then in sight while the burial service was going on, loomed large and clear before us, and our ship, rounding into the harbor, swung at her moorings. Having taken the precaution to telegraph for rooms from Tuticorin, we had no sooner come to a stand than the tall porter of the hotel met us with a note, and our immediate cares were ended. Delivering ourselves into his hands we were also delivered from the swarm of excited, shouting boatmen who surrounded our vessel, much as vultures surround a newly discovered corpse, and with much the same interest. It is not pleasant landing in a strange port on the Sabbath, as we have several times been compelled to do. But it was made as easy and quiet for us as possible, and soon we were safely and comfortably quartered in the Grand Oriental Hotel. This is a large caravansary, close to the quay and looking off upon the harbor, and constantly filled and emptied, as troops of travellers are almost daily landed and embarked. Different lines of steamers, plying to and from all parts of Europe and the East, meet here and hence diverge, and passengers exchange according to the port they seek and the route they wish to pursue. A noble breakwater, erected with great labor and expense, makes a fine harbor, in which a large fleet of steamers and sailing vessels of all sorts and sizes is constantly to be seen. Here, after tarrying a few days, we propose to resume our journey on the 29th for Hong Kong and Amoy.

COUNTRY ROAD, KANDY, CEYLON.

CHAPTER XVII.

PLEASING PROSPECTS IN CEYLON.

COLOMBO, March 23

WE have now been for eight days on this charming island. Its intense tropical beauty no words of mine can adequately describe. Even in approaching it one is deeply impressed. Dense masses of foliage crown the heights and cover the slopes, descending till they reach the narrow strip of gleaming sand which belts it. Beyond and towering above the shore line rises the mountain range which forms the backbone of the southern portion, to a height of 8,000 feet or more. Conspicuous, though not the highest, is Adam's Peak, where a depression in the rock is shown, on its very top, which devout Hindus declare to be the imprint of Shiva's foot when he stepped across from India! The Buddhists declare that Buddha's foot rested there and left its mark, while Mohammedans claim it as the footprint of Adam. Hence, probably, the name the mountain bears.

"You will like Ceylon," said one of the P. and O. captains with whom we sailed. "All Americans are delighted with it." As good Americans so were we. Barring the heat and the humidity, life here might be made ideal and idyllic. But these conditions are inseparable from its insular position, under an almost vertical sun. The influence of the surrounding ocean and its breezes give to the climate a considerable degree of uniformity. Hence all manner of tropical vegetation flourishes with great luxuriance. Towns and cities are embowered in groves of palms, breadfruit and other trees, and almost hidden from sight. No one, on landing at Colombo, would suspect the presence of a great city of 130,000 inhabitants. Portions of it, indeed, are visible enough. One, filled with the native shops and lowly homes of artisans and laborers, lies low along the eastern and southern shore of the harbor, set in a background of green. The other, containing the hotels and public buildings, lies to the south and west, embracing a slight elevation, on whose western face still stand remnants of the old city wall or fort, fronting the harbor and the sea.

Some of the buildings are fine, and the broad streets are lively with jinrikshas and gharries, and thronged with people in picturesquely varied and colored costumes. As the British government maintains a garrison here, the officers' quarters and extensive barracks cover a wide space in this part of the city, and "Tommy Atkins," in suit of white, with swinging arms and swaggering gait and Scotch cap perched on one side of his head, is a frequent and prominent figure on the streets and promenades.

A unique feature of the town is the great light-house, standing at the very centre of this section, at the crossing of two prominent streets and at the highest point. A large square clock tower bears aloft the flashing light, which can be seen eighteen miles out to sea. As the great lantern revolves by night, its flashes fall on house and street and athwart the path of wayfarers with a peculiarly weird effect. An admirable drive and promenade extend for a mile or more along the western shore, raised but a few feet above the beach and facing the sea, called "Galle Face" (pronounced *gaul*). In the late afternoon the driveway is thronged with carriages and the footway with pedestrians, seeking refreshment from the heat of the day in the cool breeze from off the water and the flashing waves as they roll in on the beach close at hand.

The city is made up of various quarters, passing under different names, and stretching out for long distances. It is only when one drives, or rides in a "riksha," through the long avenues shaded with palm groves and other trees, lined in continuous rows on either side, now with villas and gardens, and now with the small shops of every sort that give to some of them the appearance of a prolonged bazar, that he can form any conception of the extent of the city or the population that dwells within its limits. Great groves of cocoanut palms, with their clusters of nuts, rise high above the shops and cabins, and even the more pretentious houses. The broad-leaved breadfruit stretches out its branches of dark green; the jackfruit, with its curious yellow gourd like fruit growing directly from the trunk; the tall slender, arrowy areca palm, with its streaming clusters of the nuts which Hindus love to chew, when wrapped with a pinch of lime in the pungent betel leaf; clumps of graceful, feathery bamboos; all these, and more, line and shadow the roads, and among and over them creep luxuriant and gigantic vines, some of them gorgeous in bloom. When darkness comes the little shops are lighted up, and in the dense shade of the trees numerous fireflies flit and dart, unseemly sights are hidden, and the scene which was interesting enough by day becomes fascinating by night. To drive through these streets in the early evening, and then come out on Galle Face, with the sea breeze in one's face, the gleam of starlight or moonlight on the water and the rush of the waves in his ears, is an experience to be remembered.

Perhaps you expect me to quote Bishop Heber here. But I am not going to do it. Partly because you know the "Missionary Hymn" already, and have probably repeated it to yourself, and partly because I have not found "man" here—the man of the island—"vile" above many others I have seen. In fact, the vilest men I have come across since landing here were not natives at all, but drunken sailors from foreign ships, in foreign dress, perambulating the streets from dusk to midnight, and sometimes later, and making night hideous with their drunken outcries. Over and over again have I got out of bed, in the dead of night, to see what the occasion of some passing tumult might be, and in every case the cause was the same. This is the curse, or one great curse, of ports in heathen lands, not to speak of ports in lands called Christian.

The people of the island are largely, and, I believe, pretty nearly equally divided between Tamils and Sinhalese (formerly spelled Cingalese). The Tamils are Hindus, and preserve here most of the traits peculiar to the same people in India. They have their Hindu temples and worship here as there, though the bonds of caste are said to be somewhat relaxed, and the influence and prestige of the Brahmins is much less. They are the principal laborers on the tea plantations, and their numbers are largely reinforced from South India, as mentioned in my last letter. Much faithful missionary work is done among these "plantation coolies," under the most adverse and discouraging conditions. They are widely scattered, constantly changing, and, as a rule, which has its refreshing and creditable exceptions, Christian work among them is not encouraged by the planters. Some, indeed, actually discourage it, declaring that they do not wish their coolies instructed or to become Christians. Notwithstanding these obstacles, the work is faithfully and laboriously prosecuted by agents of the Church Missionary Society and others, and with a degree of success which, under the circumstances, is surprising.

The bulk of the Tamil population is found in the north,

which they inhabit almost exclusively, though they are found in large numbers in this city and others as laborers. The American Board has had a thriving mission in the north, with its centre in Jaffna, since 1815. It was my strong desire to be able to visit it, but communication is so difficult, and requires so much time, whether overland or by sea, that the hope is reluctantly abandoned.

In outward appearance the Sinhalese are readily distinguished from the Tamils, with whom they bear not unfavorable comparison in some respects, though not as regards industry. They seem to have their full share of the "inertia" so characteristic of dwellers in tropical climes. Nature is prodigal, and comparatively little supports life. Therefore they content themselves with little. A Sinhalese farmer, so I am told, who was asked why he did not raise a second crop on his land, as he might easily do, replied that one crop gave him and his family enough to eat for a year; why should he trouble himself to raise a second that he did not need? This aversion to labor, not altogether unnatural in such a climate, furnishes ground for the preference given to the Tamils as laborers. Whatever his laziness and his other defects, there is something not unattractive in the Sinhalese as he appears here in Colombo. His lighter skin; his upright, rather delicate, figure; the "repose" of his face and comparative delicacy of feature; his laudable tendency to wear "clothes," and a full suit at that, rather than a mere waist cloth, with the neatness and picturesqueness of his costume, give him an external appearance not at all unpleasing. The same indolence and torpidity which characterize him physically, are said to apply to his intellect and conscience. We found him, however, if not keen to labor, sufficiently sharp at a bargain. Characteristic of Colombo are its shops, where precious stones, gold and silver jewelry and filagree work, carving in ebony and ivory, and curios of various sorts, are exposed for sale. Here, as in all the East, the price asked in the native shops is far in excess of that which the article is worth or the dealer expects to obtain. The endless chaffer and dicker which take place before a purchase, are expected by the merchant, and form the delight of many shoppers—the weariness and disgust of others. The results are often surprising—in all cases much less than the original price being finally accepted, often so little as one-half, one-third, and not infrequently one-fourth. The buyer goes his way congratulating himself on having secured "a bargain." Perhaps he has, but the chances are that the advantage is on the side of the dealer after all.

CHAPTER XVIII.

MISSIONS AND MOUNTAIN VIEWS AT KANDY.

COLOMBO, March 28

MISSION work is carried on in Colombo by Roman Catholics and several Protestant societies. The former seem to be largely in the ascendant. Probably they have never lost the advantage given them by priority of entrance, and the forcible or otherwise unchristian methods adopted by the Portuguese for the propagation of the faith. Of Protestants, the Church Missionary Society (English) has the largest following. The English Baptists and Wesleyans are also represented by Churches and schools, together with the S. P. G.'s (Society for the Propagation of the Gospel), though the latter might object to being classed with Protestants. They and the Wesleyans have colleges, St. Thomas's, that of the S. P. G.'s being located in a park in which stands also the Anglican Cathedral. The Church Missionary Society has a college at Kandy, the ancient capital of Ceylon, and distant about seventy-five miles by rail. The native communicants connected with these various missions in Colombo number from 1,300 to 1,500. It might seem, and probably will, to some, that this is but a meagre result of labors faithfully prosecuted from the earlier part of this century. It is a sad fact—no more sad than true—that the least encouraging results of missionary effort are found in seaports like Colombo. There seems to be something in the moral atmosphere of such places, and much in close and direct contact with that phase of so-called Christianity which presents itself in official and commercial garb and relations, which renders missionary labor comparatively unproductive. While such places have undoubted advantages as centres of missionary influence and operation, they too seldom have "the smell of a field which the Lord hath blessed."

High up among the hills, at an elevation of nearly 1,700 feet above sea level, lies Kandy, the ancient capital above alluded to. Thither we went for a few days last week, to escape the extreme heat of this city and enjoy a brief breathing space among the mountains. A fine carriage road of easy grade, and also a railroad, connect it with Colombo. We took the railroad, as offering promise of easiest and most speedy transportation. Leaving the city at a station on the borders of a small but beautiful lake, the road passes through deeply shaded groves of palms and other trees, and crossing a considerable river by a noble bridge, emerges into the open country. The whole distance shows one unbroken but ever-changing scene of tropical beauty. Rich fields of rice stretch wide on either hand, in which men and women are toiling, weeding or transplanting in mud and water, or lifting the water, in buckets curiously suspended, from the ditches to flood the fields. In some the soft muddy soil is being prepared for a new crop, and the diminutive bullocks or lazy water buffalos are slowly dragging behind them the diminutive native plow. In ponds and pools the buffalos—the most hideous animal beneath the sun—are wallowing in the mud and water they so dearly love. Luxuriant groves overshadow and almost hide from view the hamlets and and single huts that seek their shelter from the scorching sun. Low wooded hills appear, through which the road winds tortuously, disclosing at each turn some new vision of beauty to delight the eye. The air is full of fragrance from flowering shrubs and vines which hang in gorgeous festoons from the loftiest trees. The stations are decked with flowers of every hue. For fifty miles the entire distance seems to lie in one vast park with blooming gardens interspersed. Then the ascent begins, from an elevation of only 300 feet, and in twelve miles the laboring train climbs to a height of 1,698 feet above the sea. Skirting the edge of many a precipice the eye looks down on smiling valleys where the lower slopes, terrace above terrace, are under highest cultivation, and brilliant with the green of growing rice, or off on ranges of glorious hills rising tier above tier, in rounded or fantastic shapes. If Adam did not live among these hills he might have done it and found Paradise.

Kandy itself is finely situated, in a bowl shut in by hills on all sides. A small but beautiful lake disputes with it possession of the bowl. At midday the sun beats down with tropical fury, and pith helmets and white umbrellas are as needful for protection from his rays as on the coast. But the air is freer and drier, and, when the sun withdraws his heat and the evening shadows settle down, delightfully cool. At night, for the first time in many weeks, we found a blanket desirable for comfort. Numerous drives and walks, laid out with skill and kept in perfect order, open the secrets of the hills and offer numerous' views of surpassing beauty. From a nucleus on the borders of the lake, the town stretches in two or three long streets, closely built and lined with shops or neat-looking cottages of stone and brick. Here are several Buddhist temples, chief among them the Malagawa temple, in which is kept one of Buddha's teeth. The casket which holds it is alone exhibited to ordinary visitors, and that only at certain hours. Those who have seen it stand surprised at its enormous size, and at the conception of the gigantic mouth that must have held it. For a consideration, the treasures of the temple are also shown. Four miles from Kandy, on the road to Colombo, are the Peradeniya Botanical Gardens, in which we spent two delightful afternoons. The road thither lies through a suburb of Kandy, long drawn out, lined on either side by shops and cottages which are surrounded by cocoanut palms, breadfruit, jackfruit, coffee and other trees. Almost, if not quite, every tree and plant known to the tropics and semi-tropical regions, is to be found in these gardens. The entrance is a bower of beauty, the posts of the gate being entirely hidden by luxuriant creepers. At the left stands an imposing row of stately India rubber trees with their thick, glossy foliage, the roots exposed and looking as though they had trickled down from the massive trunks and spread themselves in viscid streams over the surface of the ground at their own sweet will. A very intelligent Sinhalese, speaking excellent American (not English) accompanied us through the grounds and pointed out the most interesting objects. The collection of palms, from every portion of the world in which palms grow, is especially full and complete. An avenue of sago palms, rising like pillars smooth and straight to a great height, their fronds meeting overhead, formed a spectacle of surpassing beauty. There, too, was the talipot palm in all stages of growth, of vigor and decay. With larger trunk than most other varieties, it grows for years till it attains a great height, its top crowned with a cluster of wide-spreading leaves. At length from the very centre of this clump, a tall flower stem shoots up to an additional height of twenty or thirty feet. It blossoms and the flowers die, and the tall tree itself, its lifework finished, decays and falls. We saw the vigorous growth, the shooting stem, and the decaying tree—the top fallen over and hanging downward, doubling together the trunk that had borne it, from which the very heart had rotted out. There were palms from Africa—the "traveller's," which secretes at the base of its spreading fronds a cup of water to which thirsty travellers have recourse — and many others. Why should I attempt the impossible task of enumerating the hundred or more varieties? Are they not there for every one to see who will pay these gardens a visit? Specially noticeable and beautiful were the clumps of bamboo, rising from the brink of the river which encircles the garden, or set in the midst of smoothly shaven grass, and reaching a height and size I had not conceived possible. Few things in the garden, or in nature anywhere, are more beautiful than they. Orchids abound, and ferns, and flowering creepers, some of the latter of gigantic size, climbing the tallest trees and hanging from them in long streamers, or binding tree to tree in graceful festoons. The whole place is an epitome of the tropics—not in the wild and bewildering confusion of their native state, but orderly, well kept, accessible, and open to study and inspection. Even the "Deadly Upas" tree is there, innocuous, shedding no baleful atmosphere nor anything more hurtful than its withering leaves. Its juice is poisonous and that alone. But as we had no arrows to poison we did not come in contact with it.

The hillsides about Kandy, and the slopes among all these mountains, are devoted to tea-culture. Formerly much coffee was raised on these plantations, but of late years the ravages of a bug upon the leaves have been so destructive as to ruin the crops, and planters are giving their attention almost exclusively to tea. The process of culture and cure is similar in almost every respect to that prevailing in India, which I have already described. I am told that the Ceylon and India teas are rapidly displacing, in Great Britain, the teas of China and Formosa.

CHAPTER XIX.

TROPICAL SEAS AND SCENES.

HONG KONG, April 18

WE left Colombo on the 29th of March in the good ship "Ravenna." Smooth seas and cloudless skies made the voyage for several days and nights a very enjoyable one. Life on these P. & O. (Peninsular & Oriental) steamers is made as comfortable and pleasant as it is possible for life at sea to be. Awnings of double thickness cover the decks and intercept the heat by day and the rain by night. The latter item is not unimportant when fully two thirds of the saloon passengers camp down on deck, nightly, to escape the heat and closeness of the cabins in these lower latitudes. In the cooler parts of the day—morning and evening—provision is made for various sports and games, in which the ladies sometimes join. At evening the deck is lighted with electric lamps, the piano is opened, and songs and music help to while away the hours. On clear nights the stars shine with a peculiar brilliancy, the old familiar stars and constellations are largely lost to sight, and new ones take their places. Brilliant among them hangs the Southern Cross, yet not so glorious as the hope of years and the rapturous descriptions of others had led us to expect.

The one blot and shame on all these steamers—we have now been on four of them—is the daily "pool" over the day's run. Even the ladies, many of them, take their chances in this sort of gambling and win or lose their share of the stakes. There seems to be nothing, however innocent, which cannot be made instrumental in feeding the passion for gambling, which in one form or another, seems to be universal.

In the second cabin were a party of missionaries on their way to China, with whom we had some pleasant intercourse. Four of them were young men on their way to join the mission of the Wesleyan (English) Society at Hankow. This is the place where one of their missionaries, the Rev. Mr. Argent, lost his life last year at the hands of an infuriated Chinese mob. As in so many other instances has been the case, his death has served to fire the zeal of others, and prompted renewed efforts to carry forward the work in which and for which he laid down his life. Modest and unassuming, they yet showed no sign of fear in contemplation of the work and possible perils to which they were going. God grant them His protection and abundant blessing.

As we approached the Straits of Malacca the weather changed, the air grew thick and moist, dense masses of fog and cloud shut in the view, and sudden, sharp, short showers descended frequently. The atmosphere seemed that of a huge vapor bath, and existence grew burdensome. At length, early on Sunday morning, April 3d, we anchored off the island of Penang. No need to remind ourselves that we were in the tropics. The fact appealed to every sense. Perpetual summer reigns, and clothes the island with luxuriant and unchanging beauty. The town itself lies low, and shows but little to attract or interest. Behind it rises Penang Hill to a height of nearly 3,000 feet, clothed to the summit with tropical verdure. With excellent judgment and good taste the Governor of the settlement has pitched his bungalow up there, where he escapes the heat, enjoys the delightful coolness of the upper atmosphere, and looks down upon a scene of beauty—forest and sea—of which it must be hard to tire. Down the steep incline, and gleaming amid the dark greenery of the forest, leaps a beautiful cascade, distinctly visible from the steamer's deck.

Penang is one of the "Straits Settlements," as they are called, belonging to Great Britain, and has a large and rapidly growing trade, owing to its proximity to the plantations of Sumatra and the opposite peninsula of Malacca. Numerous small steamers ply between it and different points in the Straits; several lines of larger steamers connect it with Hong Kong and other ports in China, and the Great European lines make it a port-of-call. The harbor, or roadstead, is, therefore, a busy place. We did not tarry long, however, but at ten o'clock were again on our way. The confusion incident to arrival and departure prevented the usual morning service. But in the cool evening the ship's company were gathered on the deck, and joined in the English service.

The next day found us coasting along the western coast of Malacca, its wooded shores and mountain heights in constant sight. In the afternoon we entered the beautiful harbor of Singapore. Itself an island at the extreme southern end of the peninsula, its harbor is formed by other islands encircling it, and is a great naval rendezvous and coaling station. Lying almost under the equator, in latitude 1 deg., 17 min., North, the climate is subject to little change. Of its quality we had a satisfying taste, as we were able to spend the night on shore, our steamer lying over night to take in coal. The island lies low, its greatest height but little exceeding 500 feet. The city stretches for several miles along the southern shore, facing the sea. A noble Bund, flanked by the principal hotels and some fine buildings, extends along the water, and furnishes a delightful promenade and driveway. At evening it was thronged with equipages, conspicuous among them the handsome carriages, with coachmen and footmen in livery, in which wealthy Chinese merchants and their families were taking the air. While every eastern nation is represented, with many Europeans, the Chinese seem to be largely in the majority. In fact, a stranger might be excused for fancying himself in China. The language in common use is Malay, but a multitude of tongues is spoken, and one had need be a very polyglot indeed to speak and understand them all. It was interesting to come across a little neighborhood of Tamils, and a diminutive Hindu temple had a familiar if not welcome look.

In the early morning we took a drive along "Orchard Road" to the Botanical Gardens, three miles out of town. The road was excellent, as are all roads in English settlements, and from it branched off others, equally good, at frequent intervals. Trees overarched the way and darkened it with their thick masses of foliage, till the senses became weary of the shade and the dense atmosphere, and found relief in an occasional break, disclosing glimpses of the sky and letting in the air. The Gardens are of large extent, beautifully laid out, and kept in perfect order. Within them every species of tropical vegetation is to be found—trees, shrubbery, ferns, orchids, vines and flowers in endless number and variety, and of surpassing beauty. It was another glimpse of Paradise, akin and almost equal to Ceylon. Especially interesting was the house of ferns, nestling in a wooded dell, rich in varieties of "maiden hair" and delicate ferns of form and fineness we had never seen till then. Passing through the grounds and porch of Government House on our return, we were able, from the gentle eminence on which it stands, to get a view of a considerable portion of the island adjacent to the town.

Everywhere rich verdure and the densest masses of foliage, a thin vapor hanging over all, and in the distance the gleaming sea. It was a picture long to be remembered, though the atmosphere was like that of a great forcing house.

The "Straits Settlements," constituting a crown colony of Great Britain, and under colonial government, comprise Singapore, .Penang and Province Wellesley directly opposite, Malacca, with a few small and distant islands. The principal mission work is carried on by the Society for the Propagation of the Gospel (S. P. G.), though the Presbyterian Churches of England and Scotland are also represented by a small number of missionaries and stations. Within a few years work has been vigorously begun at Singapore by the Methodist Episcopal Church (North) of the United States, under the direction of Bishop Thoburn. They have a considerable force of missionaries and assistants at work among the Malays, Tamils and Chinese. The climate has proved very trying, and has interfered much with the continuance of missionaries in the field. A hospital and Anglo-Chinese College form prominent and successful features of their work.

Thick fog and rain welcomed our approach to the coast of China at Hong Kong. Moving slowly, sometimes coming to a dead stop, and then proceeding as the fog lifted a little, the good ship continually felt her way into the harbor. Huge masses of yellow earth and savage rock loomed through the mist and disappeared. Innumerable native craft of every size appeared for a moment and were lost to sight. At length the rain ceased, the clouds parted, disclosing the mountains of China and the Peak of Hong Kong on either hand, and we steamed into the harbor. And a glorious harbor it is, formed by the island of Hong Kong itself and the mainland over against which it lies, crowded with ships of every sort and size. Here lay at anchor white iron clads of different navies, and among them our own "Lancaster," in sombre black, the stars and stripes floating from her peak; a multitude of mail and merchant steamers; ships from all parts of the world; Chinese junks and Portugese lorchas, while the surface was dotted and the edge of the harbor fringed with swarms of sampans. Flitting among them, steam launches, large and small, were darting to and fro. Above it, on the south, towers "the Peak"—1,800 feet in height—one of the summits of the mountain ridge which constitutes the island of Hong Kong. The town, Victoria, rises from the water's edge and creeps, terrace above terrace, nearly half way up, by roads constructed with consummate engineering skill. Half buried among trees on the upper levels, are seen churches and other handsome buildings, and the white houses of the wealthier merchants and other residents.

Into this scene of mingled bustle and beauty we burst on the morning of the 10th. It was the work of hours to get ourselves and our belongings safely on shore and comfortably housed in the excellent "Hong Kong Hotel." Unlike many an eastern city, the favorable impression made by the view from without, is not dispelled by closer inspection from within. Created by British capital, energy and skill, and under British government, it is in many respects an English city, though inhabited by comparatively few Europeans and multitudes of Chinese and other Asiatics. Its population numbers 140,000. The streets are broad, well paved and smooth, with concrete or asphalt, well kept and clean, and lined with trees.

Along the water runs the Praya, a busy street, crowded with men and merchandise and lined with stores, hotels and offices. Next to this and running parallel to it, is

Queen's Road, the principal street of the city. Many fine buildings adorn it, conspicuous among them the elegant building of the Hong Kong and Shanghai Bank. On it stands the Clock Tower, whose bells chime the quarters, and from which distances on the island are measured. Numerous shops, both European and Chinese, along this street, display attractive wares of Eastern manufacture, especially of the arts and industries of Southern China. Silks, crapes and silverware, lacquer and porcelain, wood, ivory and bronze, are all to be found in bewildering and fascinating variety and profusion. Even in the Chinese quarters the houses are high and large as compared with the ordinary Chinese city. The contrast between this city and Canton, the largest and finest in Southern China, is very marked.

One is particularly struck with the absence of horses and wheeled vehicles of any sort, other than the jinriksha. Burdens are carried by coolies, suspended from poles and borne by one, two or more, as they may be light or heavy. On the Praya and Queen's Road the chief means of locomotion is the jinriksha, which seems to be thoroughly domesticated here from Japan. Multitudes of them are at hand, and no one need be dissatisfied either at the pace at which he is borne along, or the smoothness of the road over which he is carried. These lower streets fairly swarm with men of almost every nationality under heaven, the Chinese, of course, being the most numerous. Among them may be seen representatives from America and every nation of Europe, of various tribes of India, and from Ceylon.

For the steep inclines and higher levels, chairs alone are used, suspended on poles and borne on the shoulders of two—sometimes three—stalwart bearers, at a rapid pace. Their measured tread and the elastic spring of the poles produce a motion not disagreeable to most persons, but to some resulting in a sensation akin to sea-sickness. These inclines lead upward to roads running along the mountain side and cut out from its face, or carried over ravines by bridges and embankments. One, the Bowen road, is laid out upon the top of the Aqueduct, a noble and costly work, by means of which a supply of excellent water is brought into the city. Following its course it winds in and out along the face of the Peak for miles, at an elevation of more than a hundred feet, and furnishing a constant succession of charming views of city, mountains, harbor, and the regions opposite and beyond. But the whole town and harbor are "dominated," so to speak, by "the Peak," rising an almost perpendicular mass above them, and seeming, when one looks to the southward, to shut out the very heavens. A hard, smooth road, constructed with infinite pains and skill, climbs in many a wind and zigzag to the summit. Within the last few years a cable tramway has been added, with nearly straight course and steep incline. For a considerable distance the grade nearly approaches the perpendicular, and one involuntarily holds his breath till it is safely passed. There are large hotels on the summit, and many cottages also. To these the dwellers in the town below resort in the long, hot summer. The heat in that season is said to be intense, the great bulk of the Peak cutting the city off completely from the southwest monsoon which there prevails.

At this season, the "rainy"—and between the two monsoons—the summit is almost perpetually robed in clouds. In the eight days we have been here, but one has shown the entire mountain, clear of clouds, from top to bottom. We took advantage of this break and went up by the tramway. Though the day was warm below and the air still, the fresh breeze on the summit blew strong and chill. The view was superb. At our feet, seeming so near that we could almost toss a pebble into it, lay the city, its entire water line, stretching for miles from east to west, and all its climbing roads and terraces exposed. The harbor, thickly dotted with vessels at anchor, while innumerable steam launches and small boats — like water insects — darted or crept over its smooth surface. Hills near or far shut it in on every side. On the extreme right the Lymoon pass, but half a mile wide, opens to the ocean. Strong fortifications on either side give to the English complete control of this great artery of commerce. Over against the town lay the peninsula of Kowloon, a British possession ceded in 1861, and strongly fortified. Here are extensive warehouses or "godowns" for the storage and trans-shipment of goods, and back of all beyond the British line, the hills of China stretching away into the distance. Southward lay the ocean, its lazily swelling bosom dotted with islands and flecked with many a passing sail.

CHAPTER XX.

A FLYING VISIT TO CANTON.

HONG KONG, April 18.

CANTON, the capital of the Kwang-tung Province, is situated on the Pearl River, ninety or ninety-five miles from Hong Kong. Fine river steamers, built after the American model, ply between the two cities. The traveller who takes one of them can make it also his hotel, transferring from one to another so long as he may wish to stay. We took the "Fatshan" last Wednesday evening, and returned with her on Thursday night, finding every comfort of bedroom and table. Leaving Hong Kong at 5.30, we passed through the group of islands into the mouth of the river, guarded on either hand by frowning hills, and anchored for several hours. There are no lighthouses in the river, and the approach to Canton by night is dangerous and, I believe, forbidden. Awake at an early hour, the spectacle, as we approached the city, was novel and very interesting. It extends for about four miles along the north bank of the river. The houses, for the most part, are of one story only. Towering above them were the twin spires of the Roman Catholic Cathedral, built of solid granite, and rising to a height of 150 feet. Almost equally prominent are the pawnshops—immense square structures of granite, rising several stories above the houses and shops. They are thus built for safety and do a thriving business. Large quantities of goods are pawned, never to be redeemed, and every year a sale is made of articles thus left. Beside this use, many people bring each summer their winter wardrobes and leave them on deposit, taking thence the summer clothing which they had similarly deposited at the approach of winter. They thus become vast storehouses for people whose supply of house room is limited, as that of the vast majority of the people is.

Along the river, which is here two miles in width, on both sides are moored countless river and houseboats, in solid rows or blocks, with watery lanes and avenues between. On these boats the people who own them live, scarcely ever, some of them never, setting foot on land. The children are born, grow up and die with no other house or home. Of the 1,500,000 inhabitants of Canton, it is estimated that fully 300,000 live thus on the water. Beside these, numerous boats, similarly inhabited, are plying to and fro across the river, or up and down to points above or below. To bring a large steamboat through such a swarm without accident is no easy task, and one by which alone our captain declared he earned his salary.

Soon after reaching the wharf Dr. B. C. Henry, of the American Presbyterian Mission, came on board and kindly insisted on our coming home with him to breakfast. Both he and his family showed us no little kindness, devoting the day to our entertainment and profit. We visited the Woman's and Girls' School in the same compound, under the charge of Miss Lewis, and were delighted with the bright, intelligent faces of the native teachers and the 120 scholars in attendance. Later in the day we also visited the Hospital close at hand, first opened by Dr. Peter Parker in 1839, but now and for many years under the able conduct of Dr. Kerr. It was a disappointment not to meet the doctor, whose name is widely known in America and in China, but Dr. Swan and Miss Dr. Niles kindly supplied his place, and no attention or information were lacking. A vast amount of work is done here. During 1891 no less than 22,452 out-patients and 1,269 in-patients were treated, and 2,140 surgical operations performed. The wards are extensive, and a fine chapel affords opportunity for daily morning and evening worship and Sunday services as well. The work of the Mission is extensive, reaching far into the interior, even to the borders of Hunan, the hotbed of bigotry and hatred of foreigners, and fomenting centre of recent disturbances and riots further north. It extends also to the islands of Macao and Hainan on the south.

The old city of Canton is very ancient, surrounded by a wall—as all Chinese cities are—which was built in the eleventh century and completed as it now stands in the fourteenth. It is called, also, the City of Rams, owing to the tradition that, in the fourteenth century, or before, five Genii visited it, riding on five rams, and bearing in their hands the five principal grains, rice, wheat, etc. These they gave to the inhabitants of the city with the prayer that they might "prosper and multiply." The Genii then disappeared and the rams were turned into stone. The story must be true, for are not the stones preserved to this day in the temple erected to the five Genii, where also their images are set up, each with his appropriate stone at his feet? Their benevolent prayer, also, has been answered, for Canton is a very wealthy city, with numbers of rich merchants, and the population and dwellings have many times outgrown its original proportions. It is said that when the Roman Catholic Cathedral, with its lofty spires, was built, the people were greatly excited lest the happy relations of the spirits should be interfered with, and the prosperity of the city ruinously disturbed. The wise men, skilled in such matters, were consulted. They sagely and prudently delivered the opinion that the spires were two new horns sprouting from the rams and therefore boded no ill to the city. The spires were, therefore, allowed to stand, however illogical and unwarranted the conclusion may have been.

The city is well described as a "labyrinth of lanes." Woe to the traveller who attempts to thread its mazes unguided and alone. There is a guild of licensed guides who meet the boats and conduct strangers through the streets. We, more fortunate, saw them under the genial conduct of Dr. Henry. There is a law that no street shall be of a less width than eight feet! Few, if any, were wider. It was hard to believe that many of them were so wide. Nor do I believe it. For many times, when our chairs stopped, it would have been difficult for another chair to pass. They are paved with stone, a sewer running under the stones, from which odorous exhalations find their way upward through frequent cracks and gaps. They have curious names, of which the following are specimens: "White Rice," "Thirteen Hong," "New Bean," "Ascending Dragon," "Longevity Lane," "Great Peace," "Heavenly Peace," "Benevolence and Love." Some of them are covered, and most of them lined on either side with shops. Those of the same character are crowded together in the same street, interspersed with cook-shops, restaurants and opium dens, all contributing to swell the cloud of odors that ascend and fill the air. Some of these shops are filled with goods of elegant material and manufacture, as the jade-stone, silk and black-wood shops and many others. Gaudy signs are over the entrance, and long, swinging blocks of lacquered wood in various colors display in gilt characters an invitation to enter, or some high-sounding description of the goods to be found within, some moral aphorism or some quotation from the classics. Among the meat shops this sign hung in full view: "Nice, fresh, black pussy cat." Each shop, too, has its shrine,

EATING CHOW.

before which incense is kept burning to the god of trade.

The streets were thronged with people, and many followed our procession—chiefly curious boys—and, as often as we entered any shop, the doors and street outside were instantly filled with a curious, gaping crowd as intent on inspecting the foreign visitors as they were on inspecting the goods exposed for sale. The same was true of every temple and Pagoda at which we halted, till at last it ceased to be either laughable or annoying, and became a matter of entire indifference. It was impossible to dismiss them and useless to be annoyed by them. The only proper feeling would have been satisfaction in affording them so rare a show.

Threading the streets thus attended we visited the Cathedral of which I have already spoken, a fine building of solid granite, begun in 1860 and completed twenty years later. Its lofty nave and handsome glass windows seemed out of place in such a city. Thence to the Examination Hall, where recently 12,000 students went up for the Provincial examination, and 11,880 were "plucked." This does not, however, mean that only 120 were found worthy to pass, but that the government would only give so many degrees. We could see the long rows of barrack-like buildings in which candidates are immured in cells during the entire period assigned to the examination, but unfortunately could not enter, as a preliminary examination was in process. The Emperor's Temple, not far off, encloses a large rectangular court, comprising two pavilions, one on the north, in which the Emperor's tablet is placed, and one on the south, through which entrance is made. On the east and west sides are halls in which the mandarins assemble on the occasions when state worship is performed. The usual seasons are the emperor's birthday and the

Chinese New Year, and also when an emperor is married, but special services may be commanded at other times. The whole place was evidently much neglected, the court overgrown with grass and weeds, and the decorations had a very cheap and tawdry effect. When the proper time arrives, everything will be newly furnished, and the assembled magnates will prostrate themselves before the tablet of the Son of Heaven.

Mounting the old wall, faced with stone and brick and filled in with earth, with a width of from fifteen to twenty-five feet, we proceeded for some distance along the northeastern side, till we reached the five-storied tower or pagoda on the highest point and extreme north of the city. Ascending to the upper floor a fine view of the entire city and surrounding country spread out before us. In front a continuous map of roofs extending for miles, with no apparent divisions, such as the broad streets of a Western city would make. Behind us the hills were literally covered with graves, many of them quite pretentious, among which could be seen rows of jars containing the remains of long-buried dead—"potted ancestors," as they are irreverently styled. About the graves were many parties paying honors to the departed, laying paper and setting off fireworks to show the reverence of the living and ease the troubled spirits of the dead. Having refreshed ourselves with tea and native cakes, and the cool air, we descended again to the streets. Winding along their narrow and crooked course, stopping now at a shop and again at a temple or pagoda, we found ourselves, in mid-afternoon, again under Dr. Henry's hospitable roof. Whoever wishes to get much information, given in an entertaining way, let him get hold of Dr. Henry's book, "The Cross and the Dragon," and read it carefully. It will tell him far more than I can hope to do in these rambling letters.

We returned to the steamer in one of the riverboats of which I have spoken. For crew we had a stalwart boatman in the bow, vigorously plying the oars, and in the stern a woman, evidently his wife, handling with equal strength and dexterity a long and powerful sweep with which she at the same time steered and propelled the little craft, her means of livelihood and her home. An infant of not many months was slung on her back, between her shoulders, and as she stepped back and forth the child's head kept bobbing violently up and down. Occasionally it would graze the canvas matting, set up for a covering, overhead. It seemed as though its neck must be dislocated with every stroke of the sweep. Yet not a single cry escaped its lips, and it bore all the shaking with true Chinese stolidity. Much practice had, no doubt, made it perfect in patience.

In the midst of these strange surroundings in this far-off land, it was a pleasure to recognize our kind friends waving their farewells from their verandah which overlooks the river.

CHAPTER XXI.

MISSION HOMES AND SCHOOLS IN CHINA.

KOLONGSU, AMOY, April 26

We have now been here five days, having left Hong Kong on the 19th, and arrived here on the morning of the 21st. Our advent, as at Hong Kong, was made in the midst of thick fog, through which we slowly made our way, the steam whistle constantly blowing at intervals of a few seconds, and answered by the firing of guns from the different lighthouses as we passed. The use of cannon is here substituted for that of fog horns and bells as more satisfactory. The sound is certainly less dismal and aggravating than that of the horn, beside being periodic instead of continuous, thereby having the advantage.

The little steamer "Fokien," of only 500 tons, brought us in safety, but gave us a most disagreeable and thorough shaking up, and inside out, for the first twelve hours. No sooner had we emerged from the smooth water of the harbor, through the narrow Lymoon pass, than we were met by a stiff breeze from the northeast, and a sea that rolled in heavily from the Pacific. The consequences were by no means agreeable, and those who had successfully braved the Atlantic and all the other seas we have crossed succumbed to this. Early the next morning we found ourselves sailing smoothly up the Han River to Swatow. This is an open port and town of considerable size, specially noted for the manufacture of pewter ware and a peculiar kind of fan. Its trade is large, as evidenced by the number of steamers and native boats lying at anchor. It serves, also, as a port for the very much larger city of Chow Chow Fuh, much farther up the river, to which foreign vessels are not allowed to proceed. Cargoes are broken here and carried up to the larger city in native boats. One singular article is brought in large quantities from Shanghai—pressed cakes of beans, in shape not unlike a thin grindstone or dairy cheese. Whole ship loads of these cakes were being discharged—to be sold into the country, broken up and used as a fertilizer.

Our chief interest lay with the Missions here, though we were able to visit but one of them, that of the English Presbyterians on the Swatow side. The compound in which the missionaries live is on the north bank of the river, a half mile, perhaps, below the city. It encloses several comfortable residences, with pleasant grounds about them — shaded with trees and beautiful with flowers—a considerable hospital, thronged with patients at the time of our visit, under the charge of Dr. Lyall, and schools for boys, girls and women. This station is the centre of an extensive work, reaching a wide field in the interior, and extending northward till it meets the work carried on by missionaries of the same Church from Amoy. We were most cordially received by Dr. and Mrs. Lyall, Mr. Maclagan, Miss Ricketts and others of the Mission, were shown through hospital and schools, and thus spent some pleasant hours. The American Baptists have their station nearly opposite, on the south bank of the river, which is here a mile or so in width. The time at our disposal did not admit of a visit to them also. There is a peculiar heartiness in the welcome extended by missionaries to those likeminded with them, which is worth going far to receive and is a deprivation to lose.

The city of Amoy lies on an island of the same name which, together with several smaller islands, forms an extensive harbor on the southern coast of China, opposite the mouth of the Lun Kiang or Dragon River, or River of Nine Dragons. The inner harbor is formed by the island of Kolongsu opposite the city, making an excellent land-locked port for the considerable commerce centering at Amoy. On Kolongsu the missionaries and other foreign residents have their homes. It is a rocky island of very irregular surface and outline. Numerous low peaks rise from it, covered with singular groups of rocks in all sorts of fantastic shapes and arrangement (or confusion), and crowded with the dwellings of missionaries, merchants, consuls and others. Very few foreign residents are found on the other, or city, side of the harbor. The distance across it is not great, while the freedom from odors and noises peculiar to a Chinese city would be worth securing by a much greater effort. Seen from the water, or from the opposite shore, Kolongsu presents a very attractive appearance. Scarcely had we reached our moorings last Thursday morning, when we observed two harbor boats, or sampans, rapidly pulling toward us from Kolongsu. Their near approach disclosed the familiar faces of nearly every able-bodied member of the Mission. What smiling faces they were! What happy greetings followed on deck! With what alacrity we surrendered ourselves to this boarding party, and accompanied them to the hospitable homes that had been so long waiting for us!

A nearer acquaintance, grown more perfect in the passage of several days, has not served to dispel our pleasing impressions of this island home. The Mission houses are admirably placed on high ground, looking off upon the water to the west and south. Though quite elevated, the sound of the waves breaking on the shore below is constantly in our ears. It has a soothing, cooling sound, especially in the hot, breathless, steaming nights when sleep flees from one. Most of the houses are sheltered and shaded by groups of trees, banyan, mango, pomelo and others, and the enclosures brightened and made fragrant with many flowers. Roses and heliotrope, etc., load the air with their perfume and delight the eye with their abundant beauty. Scattered over the island are groups of banyans, or single trees of immense girth and widespreading branches, affording dense and extensive shade. In the valleys and on the lower slopes are several Chinese settlements or villages, which are gradually encroaching on the foreign quarters, making the approach to some of them anything but agreeable to the senses of sight and smell. Fairly good roads and paths connect the different residences and settlements, and encircle the island, making fine promenades at evening when the weather and temperature permit. Every nook and corner capable of cultivation is planted with rice or taro, or sweet potato, or some other article of food, even little patches and terraces in almost inaccessible spots on the hillsides being made available by the patient industry of these indefatigable Chinese farmers and gardeners.

Great stretches on the hills and among the rocks are devoted to quite another sort of planting, being filled with graves. They intrude everywhere, even in the midst of the fields, and are found in the compounds of foreign residents. They are regarded with superstitious reverence, and their ubiquitous presence makes the purchase of land difficult, and often impossible. The day of our arrival, and those immediately preceding and following it, were sacred to the memory of departed ancestors, and the graves, all over the island, were strewn with paper, representing money, clothing, etc., deposited there for the use of the spirits of the deceased. They produced a singular "mussy" and shabby effect, which only wind and weather are allowed to alter or remove.

In this "Jubilee Year"—for it is just fifty years since David Abeel came up from Macao to Amoy, immediately after the close of the great war and the opening of this port to foreign residence and trade—it has been interesting to trace the beginnings of the flourishing missionary work now carried on here. British troops then held this island, and Mr. Abeel established his house upon it, together with Mr., afterward Bishop, Boone, and a Dr. Cummings, and here began the preaching of the Gospel. In 1844 he was joined by Doty and Pohlman from Borneo, where they had been laboring among the Chinese. They also resided here for a time. But sickness broke out among the troops, the island was deemed unhealthy and not fit for residence, and they took up their abode in the city opposite. The houses are still standing, though in a somewhat dilapidated condition, just on the water's edge, which they occupied. Closely shut in on every side but the water by Chinese houses, with a jetty, or landing place for boats, at the foot, and the passage leading up from it into the city beneath the verandah, they must have found life here anything but quiet and attractive. Of the sights, sounds and smells with which they were brought into close and constant contact by day and by night I shall speak farther on. A mile or more to the north are the houses built and occupied by Dr. Talmage and Mr. Rapalje in the early days, with similar surroundings, and not having the advantage of looking out upon the water. These have since been incorporated in the hospital of the English Presbyterian Mission, now presided over by Dr. Macleish, and frequently visited by the Misses Talmage for the purpose of conversation with the patients, and their instruction in the Word of Life.

To the inquiry, where did David Abeel live? no one

could give answer. At last an aged disciple was found who had been a believer more than forty years, had known that sainted man and first heard the Gospel from his lips. Under his conduct we found the place on Kolongsu. A regular Chinese house of the better class, but little altered from its former state, it stands on the edge of a small pond, beneath the shade of an immense widespreading banyan, which then, as now, covered it with its protecting branches. The old lady who occupied it would not let us in, as there was "no man in the house." But through the open bars of the gate we could see the house, on the opposite side of the little court, with wide open doors, standing just as it did in those early days, inviting entrance. A small room, on either side of the main house, was used for bedroom and for retirement. In this house, our conductor, with many others, first heard the Gospel message. It seemed a hallowed spot, notwithstanding its present occupancy, and it was hard to repress the wish that possession might in some way be regained, and the Gospel again heard within those walls. Across the little pond the house was pointed out where Bishop Boone lived, and another where they were accustomed to take their meals together.

The expectation of our coming has awakened the deepest interest, we had been told, among the Native Churches—an interest which began to manifest itself immediately on our arrival. We had scarcely found domicile with Mr. and Mrs. Van Dyck, in the house built by Dr. Kip and long occupied by him, when a deputation was announced from the Second Church of Amoy, the Church of Tek-chu-ka, as it is called. The delegation consisted of the pastor and several prominent members and officers of the church, bearing the salutations of the brethren and an earnest invitation to visit them. It was also intimated that we should be invited, in due time, to partake of a regular Chinese feast to be had in honor of our visit and of the Jubilee Year of missionary work at Amoy. Similar deputations and invitations have been pouring in upon us. No day but Sunday has been without them. The pleasure of the brethren is plain to be seen, and our own pleasure in meeting them no less. Here, as in India, I have been much impressed by the native pastors as a body. Their open, intelligent countenances, manly bearing, courtesy of manner and evident interest in their work make their appearance very pleasing, and the reports I hear of many of them confirm the impression. Some of them would be men of mark anywhere, able, I should judge, to hold their own in many respects with many American and European preachers whose advantages have been far greater. Nothing would give me greater satisfaction than to be able to present some of these men —with those in India of whom I have written, to the General Synod at its approaching session, as illustrations of the best fruits of the work the Church has been doing in these Eastern lands. I am sure that the "object lesson" would be both encouraging and inspiring.

Kolongsu is not only the place of residence for all the missionaries at Amoy—our own, the E. P.'s (English Presbyterian), and L. M. S. (London Missionary Society) —but has also the training institutions maintained by these different bodies. The advantages of such an arrangement are considerable. The scholars find a healthy location, removed from the evil influences, both physical and moral, of the city, while the missionaries have their work close at hand, and their students under their own eye and easy inspection. Each Mission has its own independent school for girls and women. Our own and the E. P. are united in the education of boys and young men in the Middle and Theological Schools. In this department the London Mission is still independent, and likely to remain so for various reasons.

It was a happy fortune, or Providence, which put our Mission in possession of the grounds purchased for the Middle School through the funds secured by Mr. Pitcher two years ago. They crown a considerable knoll, almost in the centre of the island, and the building now upon them is quite conspicuous from the harbor and from many points on the island. For the present, and until additional means can be secured for the erection of a large building adapted to school purposes (sure to be needed soon), it serves the use to which it is now put measurably well. When the new building is obtained, with moderate changes it will make an admirable home for the teacher who may have special charge of the School, and for whose advent the Mission still wait and long and pray. Is there no man in the Reformed Church, of normal training, experienced in teaching and management of schools, well up in the sciences, whose love for Christ and the souls of men would lead him to seek such a field of usefulness as this? A more important one can scarcely be found anywhere, though its pecuniary rewards offer little attraction to a man so qualified. His reward will be on high, in souls saved and characters moulded into Christian excellence and beauty, and within, in the satisfaction of helping to train the minds and develop and inspire the lives of the men who are to be largely the instruments in seeking to turn the millions in this part of China to the Lord Jesus Christ.

The Theological School has a fine new building of its own, half a mile distant from the Mission School, erected by the E. P. Mission, and is presided over by Mr. Thompson, of that Mission, Mr. Fagg having part in the instruction. A fine and promising band of young men, representing both Missions, are gathered here in preparation for the work of the ministry. In the Middle School there are at present about thirty boys. A goodly number of these are Christian boys, and some of them are looking forward, and on the way, to the Theological School. It was a great pleasure, the day after our arrival, to visit both these schools and address to them a few appropriate words.

The house erected by Dr. Talmage, and long occupied by him, is now the home of his daughters, as well as of the two young ladies, Misses Cappon and Zwemer, who arrived last fall. At only a short remove from Dr. Kip's, its situation is about equally desirable, and both are easily visible by one entering the harbor. It contains within the walls of the compound the Girls' School, the Woman's School and the old building formerly occupied by the Middle School. The ground descends so abruptly that each stands on a different level, no one encroaching on or interfering with any other, yet all within convenient compass and easy reach. Ascending from the foot of the hill, we come first to the Woman's School, where a constantly varying number of women and a few girls are gathered for a few months' instruction. A stay of a few weeks, even, is sufficient to enable the more intelligent of them to read the Scriptures in the Romanized colloquial, while reading in the character would have been forever impossible. In this and multitudes of ways this method of printing the colloquial dialect proves of inestimable advantage to the work of the Mission. Old women and young girls vie with each other in learning to read, and it was not easy to say which read with the greater freedom.

A flight of stone steps leads up to the Girls' School, an object of interest to so many, young and old, in the home land. The building is good, but not nearly large enough for the best arrangement of the school. It should some day, and that not distant, be considerably enlarged, or another and larger substituted for it. There is not room enough properly to provide for the forty-seven girls now in attendance, to say nothing of the possibility of future growth. I wish the friends at home could have seen the bright and happy faces of these girls as we saw them, and hear their recitations and songs as we heard them. Their practice under the Tonic-sol-fa system, in which they have been drilled by Mrs. Kip and Mrs. Fagg, and under Mrs. F.'s conduct, was very creditable. No wonder they seemed bright and happy, for the days spent here are among the happiest they are ever likely to see. Yet all their future will be the brighter by reason of the influence here exerted over them, and the lessons and training here received. Those who are best qualified to judge tell me, what I am quite ready to believe, that it is easy to recognize in distant parts of the field, in town and village, the women who, as girls, have had their training in this School. The influence of such women in a heathen neighborhood cannot be slight, and must be blessed. I will reserve Amoy city and island for another letter.

CHAPTER XXII.

UP THE LUN RIVER BY SAIL AND POLE.

Sio-Khe, April 30

SINCE my last date we have made a trip to Sio-Khe, and thus fulfilled one of the strongest desires I had in coming to China. When the accounts of troubles in the North reached us, I began to fear that the country about Amoy might be so disturbed as to render such a tour inexpedient or impossible. I find, however, that in this part of the Province of Fokien there has been no disturbance whatever on the part of the people, and no uneasiness on the part of the missionaries. They have travelled as freely as ever, equally without molestation and without apprehension of evil. There seems to have been no change in the feeling of the people towards them, which is generally kindly, and, at the worst, curious or indifferent. Indeed, our brethren were quite amused by the letter of Consul Bedloe in regard to their heroic conduct. They were not aware of any emergency requiring such a display of heroism as was therein ascribed to them. At the same time, should such an emergency arise, I have no doubt it would be met courageously by every one of them.

To make the trip proposed it is necessary to prepare and carry bedding, cooking utensils and food, there being no provision of such things by the way. To be sure, there are Chinese inns or hotels to be found. But the accounts received of these were by no means inviting. Our missionaries never use them when it is possible to avoid it. As this trip is made altogether in boats, it was not necessary in this case. Having, happily, had no experience of the hotels, I will venture on no description of them.

The first twenty miles of the journey were made in the "Gospel Boat," a large sail boat—or small sloop—of perhaps ten tons, with a cabin accommodating comfortably two persons with their goods, and, on a pinch, making room for four. This boat is used for all preaching excursions in the harbor, and to points within twenty miles of Amoy. In consequence of the great rise and fall of the tide—from fifteen to eighteen feet—and the strong current, it is necessary to take advantage of the tide, going up with the flood and returning with the ebb. This makes it very inconvenient often, and occasions much delay. Progress in any event is generally slow, and much valuable time is consumed. I could not but feel, and say, that a steam, or naphtha, launch would be a great advantage to the brethren and to their work. To my surprise I found that the use of such launches is forbidden to foreigners. Some years ago the E. P. Mission had a steam launch, and were using it to great advantage, no Chinese questioning their right so to do. But there happened to be a foreign gentleman (?) residing here who had an antipathy to missionaries. He complained to the authorities that these missionaries were violating the treaty in making use of steam. It proved to be a fact that steam was not allowed by treaty. He professed to show, and the authorities to see, that its use by foreigners was a menace either to the trade or the safety of the Empire, and the result was the suppression of the harmless little craft and an interdict on all others. By a sort of poetical justice the interdict was probably made more comprehensive than the originator designed, and made to apply to all foreigners, consuls, merchants and others, as well as missionaries. The restriction is felt to be burdensome, but there seems no possibility of its removal without a change in the treaties. So much harm one evil-disposed person has it in his power sometimes to do. We did not bless him.

The state of the tide required that we should go on board in the evening, just as the flood began, so that we might have the full benefit of it as far as Chioh-be, about twenty miles from Amoy. The evening was mild and clear, with a gentle favoring breeze. We sat on deck and watched the sun go down, the stars come out—Jupiter in full glory casting a beam of light across the water—the shadows deepening on the river and the hills that shut it in on either side, till Chioh-be was reached at 10 P.M. There it was necessary to change from the "Gospel Boat" to one of lighter draft. For this we waited till morning, sleeping quietly in the midst of a swarm of Chinese boats. Rising early, and taking an early breakfast, we went on shore.

Chioh-be is an out-station of our Mission, having a neat chapel, which is too small and otherwise inconvenient for the congregation, but now in process of alteration and enlargement. The town was visited by David Abeel fifty years ago, and its horribly dirty condition was dwelt upon in his diary. It has not changed for the better since. The odors were ineffable—the filth indescribable. One wonders how life can be supported and health maintained in the midst of such abominations as would produce a pestilence and a panic in any American or European city. Each street leading up from the river is a sewer, covered with granite blocks, with a space between them, into which the water runs freely when it rains, and out of which the most potent odors exhale. Parallel with the river, at a distance of about an eighth of a mile, runs—or rather stagnates—a wide, open sewer, filled with a dense, reeking, black fluid mass. On either side of it is a narrow walk, lined with shops. Business and traffic goes on, and the people pass and repass, or stand in knots and groups, apparently utterly oblivious of the foul nuisance under their very noses. Piles of rubbish and garbage are heaped up in every convenient corner of the narrow streets, and other offences which cannot be mentioned here cry to heaven. Their offence is rank.

Crossing this ditch, and proceeding some little distance further through this carnival of dirt, we made our way to the chapel. This is a native house arranged for the purposes of Christian worship, the main room being the audience room for men, while a smaller, in the rear of the pulpit, and cut off by a high screen, is set apart for the women. One could not but pity them, thus shut up in a pen, and able only to see the preacher's back. The pastor was absent, but we found an elder and a few members just making ready to visit us on the boat. They gave us a hearty welcome and accompanied us to the old city or fort. In every Chinese city there is such an enclosure, with high walls, and filled with houses, marking the original town, though often, as here, outgrown many times by the houses which surround it.

The walls of the fort were of stone, about twenty feet in height, and ten to twelve feet thick, filled in with earth. Great banyan trees had taken root in the soil on the walls and in the crevices between the stones, and, reaching down for moisture and nourishment had completely encased great portions of the surface of the outer wall from top to bottom. On one corner there had evidently been a tower of brick. The roots of these trees had so interpenetrated the walls and interlaced themselves that, though the bricks had almost entirely disappeared, the tower still remained, an almost perfect square wrought by nature out of banyan roots.

The effect was most surprising and altogether unique. Our friends attended us to the river, as did also a wondering, chattering crowd who had followed us to the fort. Transferring our goods to the "River boat," we bade them farewell, promising to stop and meet the people on our return, and proceeded on our way, thirteen miles further, to Chiang Chiu. The breeze was light but favorable, so that the long rectangular sail of grass matting was hoisted. But the current was strong, and oars and poles were plied constantly beside. The sky was bright and the air delightfully cool and fresh. Great numbers of boats were going up or coming down, some loaded with merchandise of various sorts, and some filled with passengers, to whom our appearance afforded an occasion of interest and merriment. Their heads were stretched out to get as near and long a view as possible of the foreigners, and witticisms were evidently exchanged at our expense.

I was not at all prepared to find the scenery in this part of China so beautiful. The plains stretching away on either side were clothed with flourishing crops of rice and other vegetation. The banks were dotted, and sometimes lined, with clumps of graceful feathery bamboos or spreading banyans. At short intervals we passed village after village, their white walls gleaming through the thick shade of trees, many of them in most attractive locations, and, at a little distance, inviting in appearance. On either hand rose hills, wooded, or terraced and cultivated to the very summit, and still beyond them, blue and hazy in the distance, ranges of glorious mountains, with pyramids and jagged peaks.

About four hours brought us to Chiang Chiu, a large city of more than 150,000 inhabitants. There is a church here, with a small additional chapel, on one of the principal streets, and on the court a preacher's house and also several rooms for the accommodation of missionaries on their visits. These rooms were originally fitted up for the occupancy of Mr. Fagg, who was stationed here for some months. It has for many years been the earnest desire of the Mission that this city should be occupied permanently as a station by at least one missionary and a single lady to work for girls and women. The London Mission have two families here, with houses on the lower or eastern side, and a hospital under the care of Dr. Fahmy. But the city is large—quite large enough for another station, without any interference of one with the other, and is, beside, the centre of an important region where we have a growing work. This work might be greatly extended were a missionary family permanently resident. The plains contain a multitude of thriving villages, many of them larger than Sio-Khe. The city itself, formerly of much larger size, was greatly damaged by the Taiping rebellion—the long-haired rebels, as they were called—in 1865-6. But it is now beginning to recover, and rapidly increasing in population and importance. After meeting the brethren in the church and exchanging salutations with them, and offering a few words of Christian counsel and encouragement, I climbed with Mr. Rapalje and Dr. Kip the hill which overlooks the town. We looked down upon the city, a compact mass of houses stretching far away, only a small portion of it enclosed within the walls. A half-hour's chair ride through it served also to show its size and great population. Outside of it a wide plain, with wave on wave of verdant foliage, screening and sheltering innumerable villages of active, industrious people. There could be, and there is, no question in my mind that here is a most desirable spot to plant a mission station. All that is needed for it is a house and a family. Will the Church provide them? The church here, and this teeming population, have waited long for them. They should wait no longer.

Above Chiang Chiu the river becomes tortuous and shallow. The boat in which we had come thus far could not ascend further, and we had, therefore, to change to still another, of exceedingly light draft and peculiar construction. A picturesque bridge, with stone piers and many spans, and shops on either side, crosses the river at Chiang Chiu. One of the piers stands on a small island crowded with houses. On this island we found the up-river boat waiting for us in the early morning. A long, shallow, flat-bottomed affair it was, with rounding sides and narrowing toward either end, but with blunt bow and stern. Over it was a rounded covering of palm-leaf matting on bamboo frame, made in sections and telescoped, one section within another. These could be drawn out till the whole length was thus covered and protected from sun or rain. Except at night, however, the foremost and rear sections were not drawn, thus leaving a portion of open deck at either end. The first thing after going on board was to take off our shoes! However dirty the Chinese houses may be—and their dirtiness is unspeakable—the boats are scrupulously clean. The next thing was to look about us, and this had to be done from a sitting posture, as it was impossible to stand erect beneath the covering. The boat was commanded by a vigorous old woman, seventy-two years of age, as she informed us! For crew there were her daughter, son-in-law and a hired hand. The daughter's children, four in number, composed part of the company, for this was their only home. All the conveniences of home were there also—a little furnace for cooking, the smoke from which, drifting sternward, almost blinded us when the family meals were being prepared, sundry pots and kettles, baskets and beds. Nor was this all, for lifting up one of the deck planks forward disclosed a litter of rabbits, and still another, the inevitable family pig! Every Chinese house has one or more—why not the house boat? There he lay under the deck, from daylight till dark, scarcely uttering a sound, and only rising when the plank was lifted that he might be fed. That the home might not want adornment, two or three pieces of red paper, printed in Chinese character, were pasted against the palm-leaf walls, and two or three potted plants reposed securely on a shelf in the bow. The Chinese are great lovers of flowers, and of the numerous boats we passed scarcely one lacked the pots and plants.

Thus equipped we started off at six. Our method of progression was by poling. All four hands took part in it, and kept it up, with brief intermission for rest and food by each in turn, for sixteen hours, for it was ten o'clock in the evening when we tied up for the night at Soa Sia, having laboriously accomplished eighteen miles! It seemed impossible that human muscles—to say nothing of women's—could hold out so long. Yet this is their life, and probably it was an easy day for them, as the boat was light.

The city stretches for some distance along the north bank of the river. Troops of boats were coming and going, with loads of people or merchandise, crockery, wood, bricks, country produce, what not? The river bed was wide and winding, and the shallow channel wound again from side to side within it—like a snake within a snake—and frequent shallows caused many stoppages, with many shouts and groans. Often a dozen boats would be stranded together. The boatmen, habited in the scanty costume which Chinese laborers of all classes so much affect, finding all efforts with the poles utterly useless, jumped overboard, and, putting their shoulders to the work, fairly lifted the boat off and sent her forward into deeper water. Over and over again, during this and the following day, was this expedient resorted to. From all this it will be readily believed that poling up a Chinese river is no easy matter—for the polers.

The rivers are the great highways of China. Of roads, properly speaking, they have none. The best, in these parts at least, are only a few feet wide, paved sometimes with jagged stones. Most of them are simple ridges winding in and out among the fields. Transportation over them is done exclusively on the shoulders of men, at least in Southern China, and such a thing as a wheeled vehicle is not to be seen anywhere, or a beast of burden. Hence, the value of the boat and the river. Hence, also, no doubt, the numbers of people who find their living and make their homes on the water.

The scenery through which we passed was not less interesting and charming than the day before. High mountain ranges appeared on either hand, sometimes at a distance, and sometimes closing in upon the river which wound its way between them. Peculiar low hills appeared, conical or pyramidal, terraced to the very top, each terrace affording space for cultivation. Here and there a temple, nestling amid shady groves, was perched on the hillsides. Large round and square towers, with strong walls, refuges of different clans in troublous times, stood half-ruined and falling to decay. A changing but ever beautiful panorama of villages and verdure unrolled itself on either side. The day was clear and bright after the clouds of the early morning had lifted. Toward noon a favoring breeze sprang up, and a tall mast was quickly lifted, on which was raised the high square-cut sail. Looking across the bends in the river, long processions of these sails could be seen above and below, looking like "an army with banners." Hour after hour passed. The evening shadows came. The mountains hung above us dark and frowning. The boatmen seemed to feel their influence, and their cries were hushed. Scarcely a sound was heard but the plashing of the poles, the rushing of the rapids, and the cries of night birds. At last a welcome light was seen, and we drew up to the landing at Soa Sia, wearied with the long journey, and glad in the hope of rest. Amid the barking of many dogs, and the scrutiny of the few villagers who happened to be abroad, we made our way to the chapel and found entrance and welcome and a good night's rest.

The Mission premises at Soa Sia consist of a commodious chapel, preacher's house, and rooms for visiting missionaries, surrounding a court with a high wall, and all substantially built of brick. All these are the result of a legacy bequeathed to Dr. Kip by a trusted serving woman, for many years in the family of a near relative. She, doubtless, had and could have but little comprehension of the good that should flow from her gift of faith and love. In the early morning we met the brethren of the church, immediately after breakfast, and then proceeded on our way. I believe the meaning of Soa Sia is Mountain City, and certainly it is rightly named. Its mountain environment, dimly seen by night, was clearly revealed by daylight. In the darkness we had left the main river and toiled for several hours up a smaller tributary stream. It had led us into a mountain valley, rugged yet beautiful. In the early morning clouds hung thick upon their summits, but were soon eaten up by the warm sun. Then the mountains stood out in bold relief against the clear sky. Slipping easily down stream, with rudder, oar and pole all plying, we reached the river in less than half the time occupied in the ascent. Then began the old toil of poling up against the current and over the shallows, the wind this time drawing ahead and making our sail useless. As we went on the shallows became more frequent and the toil increased. The boatmen struggled mightily with their poles. One in particular would brace his feet against a stiff plank lying athwart the boat, throw his whole weight upon the pole, and push until he lay almost flat on his back upon the deck, at the same time uttering a prolonged and dismal groan that would have done credit to a case of billious colic or a guilty conscience. Frequently we came upon little groups of water buffaloes, wallowing in the shallows or lying in deeper water with nothing but their ugly heads exposed. Boys in large round hats with pointed top stood guard over them, or splashed them with water, to their evident and intense delight.

About five o'clock we reached a little village, Toa-loteng, six miles from this place, where a house has been secured for a chapel. Here our long boat ride ended. Dr. Otte met us with warm greeting, and we took our places, for the rest of the way, in the sedan chairs he had provided. Lifted up on stalwart shoulders, and emerging from the village, the full beauty of the valley burst upon us like a revelation. An emerald sea of rice stretched away till it broke upon the foot of the environing hills. Islands of deeper green—groves of bamboos, banyans and other trees—enclosing numerous villages, dotted its bosom, and beyond, on every side, before, behind, the encompassing mountains on which the shadows of evening were beginning to fall. The shadows deepened, and darkness was settling down when we reached this place and were at our journey's end, having come sixty-eight miles in three days and three nights! Beneath the folds of "Old Glory" waving in the breeze, and with sound of firecrackers, we were welcomed to this inland home.

NEERBOSCH HOSPITAL, SIO-KHE, CHINA.

CHAPTER XXIII.

HOMES, HOSPITAL AND HOSPITALITY AT SIO-KHE.

KOLONGSU, Amoy, May 5

We spent nearly four—three full—days at Sio-Khe, in the delightful society of Drs. Kip and Otte and their families. From the frequency and prominence with which its name has been brought before the Church, it might be thought that Sio-Khe is a large town. It is not. Rather, it is a large village of some 5,000 or 6,000 inhabitants. Its value as a Mission Station lies in the fact that it is a convenient centre of operations, from which to reach the population of this and contiguous valleys. These embrace a large number of villages. Through evangelistic efforts and the influence of the Neerbosch Hospital, the truth is making its way among them.

Our first visit was paid to the hospital on the morning after our arrival. It adjoins Dr. Otte's house, from which its court is separated by a wall, and is of two stories, built of brick and roofed with tile, as are all buildings here. On the ground floor are the receiving and waiting room for patients, the chapel, dispensing room and dining-room, all opening out of the Doctor's office in which he sees his patients. The arrangement is ingenious and convenient. Besides these the ground floor has also a woman's ward. Other wards and rooms for the Doctor's students, are on the second floor. The wards were furnished partly with wooden beds after the Chinese pattern, and partly with neat iron bedsteads. The latter are so much easier to keep clean and sweet that the Doctor intends to use them throughout, as soon as a full supply can be obtained. At the extreme south end is the Opium Refuge, where one wretched man was undergoing treatment for relief from the terrible opium habit. In his desire for a speedy cure, he had taken in one dose the medicine prepared for three days. It was pitiful to hear him plead for more. This refuge was built in great part by the aid of the civil mandarin of the place, who has shown great interest in the hospital and its chief.

The scrupulous cleanliness which prevailed throughout was quite refreshing, and quite different from the condition of other hospitals I have seen in China. In most of them the patients provide their own food, and cook it themselves, in their own way. Utterly unused to cleanliness at home, they cannot be taught it here, when cooking and eating are concerned. To obviate this difficulty, all food is provided by the hospital, for which a charge of a few cents a day is made, simply to cover the cost. The result has been all that could be expected, though the attendance was diminished for a time.

The seven students under Dr. Otte's care and instruction are an interesting band of young men, all of them Christians. Their countenances are bright and intelligent, their manners pleasing, and their spirit earnest, manly and Christian. The doctor is very fond and—shall I say?—proud of them, and with justice it seemed to me. If they retain their Christian principle and purpose they cannot but prove valuable helpers in days to come. At the time of our visit there were not so many patients as usual. The season is an unusually busy one, and "everything that has hands and feet is in the rice fields." In a few days, however, this pressure will be lightened; people will have time to attend to their ailments, and the wards fill up. The difficulties of medical practice are immense, owing to the ignorance of the people of the simplest laws of health, their foolish and superstitious notions in regard to the body, disease and its remedies, their unwillingness or inability to comprehend or comply with the directions given them, and the universal addictedness to dirt. Of this an instance was given us, extreme perhaps, but illustrative. A man presented himself in such a condition that the doctor told him he could not treat him till he had washed himself. " Wash ! " that was a thing not to be thought of, and he refused. Treatment was therefore declined. As he kept on pleading, and was really in a suffering condition, the doctor placed him under the influence of ether, had him washed, and then proceeded with his examination and treatment. Somewhat similarly, a missionary friend tells me that he was one day sitting in a hospital when a man came in and presented his arm for treatment. He noticed that it was covered with dark brown scales, somewhat after the manner of the scales of a fish. " What is that ? " asked he of his medical friend, supposing it to be some new form of disease. " Dirt," was the concise reply. He then turned to the would-be patient and asked how often he washed. For answer, " once in ten or twenty years ! " But enough of such details. These are some of the things which make life and medical practice in China not over-pleasant.

The hospital and Dr. Otte's new and comfortable house form one group of buildings. The house faces the river, which lies so low between deep-cut banks—at this season—that it cannot be seen even from the upper verandah. Yet, after heavy rains, its banks, though fifteen to twenty feet high, are overflowed and the water reaches sometimes quite up to the mission premises. The view across the river and up to the mountains on the other side is charming. About forty rods from these is another group of buildings containing, first, in the order in which we approach them the original house—a small, though very pleasant two-story building, with court shaded by fine trees—now occupied by Dr. and Mrs. Kip. Adjoining this is the house occupied by Pastor Iap—a good specimen of the better class of Chinese dwellings—and next to this the church. This is a good-sized building of brick, with a fine doorway of stone. On the south side, and opening on a narrow passage, is the street chapel, which is always kept open, with some one in attendance to receive and answer inquirers. This, of course, fronts on the narrow street. In its rear are the kitchen and other small buildings. All these adjoin and connect in one general inclosure. Between the church and the street is a small court with high brick wall and gateway. Over the chapel is the girls' school. Here, up a narrow and steep flight of steps, we found eighteen smiling, happy girls with their teacher, who gave us cordial welcome with salutations, recitations, songs and tea. It is a pity they have not better quarters. The whole upper story—about 12 or 15 feet by 25—is divided into two departments, the front for sleeping and the rear for school and living room. The windows are small, the rooms dark and dingy looking, and wearing an aspect not at all inviting to our eyes. I sincerely hope it may not be long before they have better and more cheerful quarters, capable of receiving a much larger number of scholars, who could easily be had were there room for them.*

The church was filled to its utmost capacity on Sunday — numbers of heathen crowding round the door, and the seats full to overflowing with the members of the Church and congregation from Sio-Khe and the neighboring villages. About one-third of the audience room is divided from the rest by a high screen of wood, and this

---

* It is a great pleasure to know that, by the kind activity and liberality of friends in the Woman's Board, this hope is to be fully realized, abundant funds for a new building having been provided.

smaller portion filled with women and children. The pulpit is placed against the south wall, at the end of the partition, and commands a view of both compartments, the preacher being the only *man* visible by the women. It was a "high day," both for the people and for us. I had the privilege not only of speaking to them, conveying the salutations of the churches at home and in India, but also of baptizing an old woman of 78 years, and fifteen infants—among the latter the youngest child of Dr. and Mrs. Otte. At the close of the address the whole congregation rose to their feet, while the original member, now an elder, gave us welcome, and begged us to convey to the home churches their grateful recognition of all that had been done for them, in sending them the Gospel and Gospel teachers to live among them, and also to them and to all the churches we might visit, their warm Christian salutations. It was an impressive scene throughout, and one long to be remembered. In the afternoon the church was almost equally full, for a Sabbath school which Dr. Otte conducts. Old men and women and boys and girls were all together studying the Word of Life.

On Saturday we had the pleasure of meeting, in the morning, Pastor Iap and the other preachers in this valley, and in the afternoon, at dinner, the two Mandarins of the place, civil and military, with the pastor. Pastor Iap is a fine specimen of a Chinese Christian and preacher. Tall, somewhat venerable in appearance, with an air of natural grace and spiritual refinement, he is much respected by all classes, and is a useful minister. He has a large family, and their home, which we visited in the course of the day, is a model—scrupulously neat and clean, and thus quite an exception to the rule. His wife is a gentle, lady-like woman, and seemed a worthy companion and helper to her excellent husband.

The military Mandarin is a short, stout, round-faced, jolly-looking man, continually smiling or laughing. He has been, until recently, not favorably disposed toward the hospital or the work of the Mission. Latterly, however, his attitude has changed, and he is now on friendly terms, and a contributor to the hospital. The civil Mandarin has been friendly from the first, I believe, and has shown his disposition in many ways. Partly by his aid a verandah was added to the hospital, and subsequently the Opium Refuge of which I have spoken. He has also given the doctor a pony, which he finds very useful, and in many other ways shown his kindly feeling. Neither of them, as yet, manifests any interest in the Gospel, but their hearts are in the hands of the Lord, who can turn them whithersoever He will. After greetings were exchanged, one of their first questions was as to the age of the secretary. "What is your honorable age?" is the general inquiry of politeness among the Chinese. Of course, the inquiry was reciprocated, and the result proved that the three officials were nearly of the same age, though the foreigner was somewhat the oldest. The civil Mandarin was somewhat taller than his companion—clad in sober brown, while the other wore blue—with a sedate countenance to which spectacles gave an air of additional gravity and wisdom. Occasionally his face would be irradiated by a smile.

The dinner passed off pleasantly on the verandah. As it began to grow dark the students took matters into their own hands. The verandah had been hung with lanterns of various and curious shapes, representing flowers, fish, crabs, fruit, vegetables, etc. These were lit, and then began a discharge of crackers and display of fireworks in the court below, which lasted fully an hour. The noise attracted an immense crowd outside the compound. They climbed and lined the walls, and filled the overlooking trees. Not satisfied with this, they handed up ladders to those on the wall, to be let down inside. No sooner did these reach the ground, however, than they were seized and borne away. The talking and shouting outside almost equalled the noise within, The fireworks were of many sorts, and very curious. Precisely at 9 o'clock the assembled guests were dismissed with song and prayer, the Mandarins departed in sedan chairs in much state, with attendants bearing torches and lanterns, the crowds dispersed, and quiet reigned once more.

The civil Mandarin had left a courteous invitation to the gentlemen to dine with him on the following Monday. Such an opportunity to see the inside of a Yamen, and partake of a Chinese feast, was not to be declined. Heavy rain fell Sunday night, and Monday dawned inauspiciously. But toward noon the rain ceased, and the clouds showed signs of parting. Shortly after noon we sallied forth. The chair-bearers, supposing we were in their power, demanded an enormous overcharge, and we dispensed with their services altogether, so that they took nothing from their "strike." Our way led through wet and muddy streets, and across the bed of a creek which divides the town. A bridge formerly spanned it, but was carried away by a flood last year. The government cares nothing for such things as roads or bridges. An effort was made to repair the loss by subscription, but this fell through. So there was nothing for it but to climb down one bank, cross on planks and logs, and then climb up the other side. It would be comparatively easy to restore the bridge if a pier could be built in the middle of the stream, but this the people will not permit. Why? Because the pier would be set on the dragon's back. He would be angry, turn and destroy the bridge! Nothing could more clearly illustrate both the foolish superstitions and the utter absence of public spirit which prevail in China. These stand in the way of every public improvement, and effectually block it.

We proposed calling, on the way, on our friend, the military Mandarin. As they live quite on the other side of the town from the mission premises, it was necessary to pass through long, narrow, dirty streets. A great rabble of men and boys flanked and followed us. Arriving at the gate, cards were sent in, and quickly the great, wide gates were thrown open, and we were ushered into the outer court. At the inner door the Mandarin himself came forward to meet us, all smiles and bows. On either side of this gate were rows of long-handled pikes, spears and battle axes, all highly polished. Formerly these were used in battle, but are now kept only for show. Passing through this inner gate we found ourselves in the audience chamber, or judgment hall, decorated with scrolls and carving. A square table was spread, at which we were invited to take our seats. On it were numerous small dishes, heaped high with cakes and various confections. Tea was then served, drawn in each cup, the cup covered by an inverted saucer, without milk or sugar. The polite way of drinking it is to take the cup in both hands, and, raising it to the mouth, draw in the tea *with as much noise as possible.* The louder the noise, the higher the appreciation of the attention and the tea itself. It must be owned that this was quite fine and delicate. As we sat, the attendant rabble crowded in about the doors, curiously gazing, while peeping through the chinks on either side were the women of the household. After spending about half an hour in conversation and sampling the confectionery, we rose to go. The Mandarin politely accompanied us to the gate, the rabble fleeing before us to the street.

At the civil Mandarin's we were received with similar

impressiveness, but were ushered at once into his private apartment, where tea was immediately served. The room was plainly furnished, a large, four-post bedstead occupying the inner side. The opposite side looked out upon a court adorned with trees and flowers. The walls of the room were hung with scrolls and a few foreign prints. A large Swiss music-box, set to Chinese music, was wound up, and discoursed its melodies for our amusement. We had scarcely finished the first cup of tea when a card was brought in, and, immediately following it, the military Mandarin presented himself. He brought with him a servant bearing a metallic water-pipe, which he perpetually filled, lit, and handed to his master, who took two or three whiffs only and returned it for renewal. This he kept up all through dinner.

After considerable talk on various topics, not easy of selection, dinner was announced, and we returned to the audience chamber. Here a large circular table was spread, round which we were seated, the Mandarin's son being added to the company—a pleasant-faced young man, just then at home from Fuh-Chau, where he is studying. Sixteen small dishes of fruits and confections were arranged in a circle round the table. These were as follows: Pineapple in slices, sugared limes in honey, sugared walnuts, sugar cane cut in small sections, dragon's eye or lychee nuts, small cakes flavored with peanuts, slices of banana, dried figs, dates, biscuits stamped with Chinese characters, sponge cake, fruit jelly, lozenges stamped with characters, sausage balls, gui-pe, a common fruit unknown to me, and nut cakes. No plates or knives were provided, but before each person lay a long, two-pronged ivory fork and large pewter spoon with round bowl, a small plate of peanuts, and roasted melon seeds, and tiny glass of sour rice wine. Pastor Iap was with us, and before the dinner began our host requested him to offer prayer.

The dinner consisted of fourteen courses only, the more indigestible dishes being omitted, at Dr. Otte's request, out of deference to the feebler digestive powers of the Occidental guests. Each course was brought on in a large round bowl, and set in the centre of the table. The host then pointed to it with his fork or spoon, and waited for one of his guests to dip in first. Once this was done all were at liberty to partake. As a special act of courtesy and mark of favor, the Mandarin would frequently insert his fork into some specially delicate bit and hand it to his honored guest—an attention which was hardly as agreeable as it was polite, when it involved the eating of the morsel so presented. We often longed to copy the manners of our host and his companions, and spit out on the floor what we did not like, but failed in the requisite hardihood. Chicken in various forms, fish, shrimp, eels, mussels, soups of different kinds, dumplings, eggs black with age or cooking, followed one another in no apparent order. We ate with "long teeth," and a pile of debris soon accumulated before us on the table. The repast consumed a little more than an hour, when we rose and returned to the private room. Tea was again served, and we soon took our leave with expressions of thanks and satisfaction. The two Mandarins accompanied us to the outer gate, and there bade us farewell, a great condescension and mark of special favor. Arrived at home, we found that a box of sugar cakes and a pot of sugared limes had been sent over for our further delectation.

CHAPTER XXIV.

AMOY STREETS, SIGHTS, SOUNDS AND SMELLS.

AMOY, May 16

ON Tuesday morning we prepared to return to Amoy. As our arrival, so our departure was signalized by the discharge of long strings of fire-crackers borne on a pole. Our host of the day before sent his son, bearing parting compliments. A large crowd of townspeople, students, church members and officers, with Pastor Iap, accompanied us to the river and gathered on the bank to see us off. The rains had swollen the river considerably, and the current was strong. The old lady was waiting with her boat, and we were soon on board. Bidding farewell to our kind friends, with whom we had joined in a final prayer in Dr. Otte's parlor, we cast off and floated down the stream and out of sight. The toil of the descent, as was to be expected, was much less, and our aged skipper contented herself with plying an oar, or handling a sweep in place of rudder, instead of the laborious pole. Starting about ten in the morning, we kept on for twelve hours and tied up in the darkness off the village of Thian-po.

In the early morning we went up to the village, saw the little church, and the ground recently purchased for a parsonage. Early as it was, the school was already in session, and the scholars at their work. School hours here are from daylight till dark, with an intermission of an hour, or an hour and a half at noon. Poor children! Poor teacher!

Taking to the boat again, we found ourselves at 10.30 passing under the bridge at Chiang Chiu. Here Mr.

Fagg met us with the "river boat," and Dr. Kip with Mrs. Kip and Mrs Otte, who had accompanied us thus far, took leave of us and returned to Sio-Khe. By 1.30 we were off Chioh-be, where Pastor Lim met us to arrange for a service in the afternoon, to be followed by a Chinese supper. The church was full, though a large part of the audience were heathen and stood curiously gazing and listening. The women sat directly behind the pulpit, screened from observation by a curtain, and unable to see anything but the back of the speaker's head. If any man thinks it is easy to address an audience of Chinese, mostly heathen, with no special suggestion of topic or address to which to reply, let him try it. The pastor, at any rate, spoke with ease and grace.

The supper came at five o'clock, in the pastor's house, which adjoins the church. It consisted of eleven courses, with the same side dishes of sweet things as I have already described. Here we made our first attempt in the use of chop-sticks, and it must be confessed with indifferent success. If "there's many a slip 'twixt the cup and the lip," there are tenfold more between the dish and the lip when these implements are the means of conveyance. Whoso doubts, let him try to feed himself with a pair of ivory knitting needles, held between the fingers and thumb of one hand. Nevertheless the hospitality was genuine and hearty, and the hour passed very quickly. The good people accompanied us back to our boat and speeded us on our way with many farewells. The breeze was fresh, but adverse, and we abandoned hope of reaching Amoy that evening, though only twenty miles distant. After sitting for a few hours on deck, enjoying the free motion of the Gospel Boat, and the constantly changing scenes about us, we sought our berths, and woke early the next morning at anchor off Kolongsu.

In the towns mentioned, and the villages crowded into the valleys through which we passed, there lives a population of not much less than a million, certainly. Here and there the Gospel has gained a foothold among them. But the great mass have as yet no knowledge of the way of life. For that knowledge they look to the Reformed Church in America. The responsibility for their enlightenment and evangelization is ours. The fields are white unto harvest. Oh that the laborers to care for it might be speedily sent forth!

I have, as yet, written no description of Amoy itself Two or three visits there have served to make it as easy as it ever will be. Yet I despair of conveying any impression of the reality, which is very distinct in my own mind. A Chinese city differs *toto cœlo* from any conception of a city which an American or European would be likely to entertain. Amoy is no exception. It stands on Amoy Island, surrounded by hills, or rather immense piles of boulders, some of them of gigantic size, and thrown together in indescribable confusion. Its population is, perhaps, 150,000, or, with other towns and villages on the island, 250,000. On a small concession along the harbor face stands a row of large buildings, the "hongs" of foreign merchants and the banks. Behind them lies the native city.

To visit it we take a sampan, or native boat, from Kolongsu. This boat is of peculiar construction, with narrow bow—not sharp—and broad stern. The passengers sit in the bow. Behind them stands the boatman skillfully plying two heavy oars, with which he both propels and guides the boat, with face turned towards the bow and in the direction in which he desires to go. Multitudes of these boats are plying back and forth across the narrow harbor, or lie swarming at the frequent jetties or landing places. Steamers are leaving for Fuh Chau,

Shanghai, Formosa, Swatow, Hong Kong or the Straits Settlements, or discharging the cargoes they have brought from these various ports. Numerous junks, also, from various points nearer by, are loading or discharging.

Among them all our sampan, skillfully guided and vigorously propelled, makes its way to the jetty on the opposite shore. These jetties, for there many, are long, narrow piers, built of large blocks of granite, and sloping down and out into the water, so as to be available at all stages of the tide. Let us land at that which is just above the houses formerly occupied by Messrs. Doty and Pohlman, which still stand with their ends toward, and their walls rising directly from, the water. One cannot help breathing a sigh at the thought of all they must have endured in such surroundings. Immediately the peculiar odors of the city, not "of Araby," salute us. Amoy has the reputation, I believe, of being the dirtiest city in China. I should not be disposed to doubt or dispute its "bad eminence," had I not seen and smelt Chioh-be.

Our way leads at once up a flight of stone steps, and we are plunged immediately into a labyrinth of narrow streets and alleys. A few—two or three, perhaps—have the respectable width of from five to eight feet, for short distances. In some it is hardly possible to carry an umbrella opened, and in most for two extended umbrellas to pass each other on a level would be impossible. The passage of a chair—the only carriage known—is a matter of difficulty and confusion. Way is made for it only by dint of constant outcries on the part of the bearers, and the pressing of pedestrians into the shops on either side. None of the streets are straight, the turns being often very short and sharp. In such cases the ends of the chair poles are frequently run up into the corner shops, to the discomfort, it may be, of shopkeeper or customer, and the disarrangement of goods. But all is taken in good part, as are the numerous obstructions and inconveniences which occur in these narrow streets. Were it not so, life in them and passage through them would be one perpetual broil. As it is, one must be constantly on the watch, not only before but behind, for chairs and burden-bearers, peripatetic cooks and pedlers, buckets of water or indescribable filth carried at the end of poles slung over men's shoulders. He must have a care, too, where and on what he treads, for dogs lie in wait at almost every step, heaps of garbage and refuse are in every corner, and, to crown all, the not infrequent, self-complacent and much petted pig.

This man who comes to meet us is a barber. Over his shoulder is a short pole from which is suspended his entire apparatus. This peculiar looking box contains razors, brushes, cups, etc., and serves as a seat for him who would be shaved. From the other end hangs a furnace for heating water and the vessel which contains it. It is no uncommon sight to see him plying his vocation, shaving the head of a chance customer, along the streets or roads. Here is a licensed beggar, clad in rags and beating a gong or a drum, or leading a blind girl by the hand, whose pitiable case is expected to arouse the sympathy and benevolence of the onlooker.

One of the most singular features of a Chinese town is the organization of its beggars into guilds or associations for mutual aid and protection. It is this fact that gives the single beggar a chance, for the shopkeeper, before whose shop he takes his stand and beats his little tattoo, knows well that if he refuses to give this man anything, the whole guild will be down upon him. So, when he has endured this noise and importunity as long as he dares or cares, he flings a cash, and so purchases peace for a season.

Most of the streets through which we pass are lined on either side with shops. Some of these—on one or two principal streets—are of fair size and appearance. As in other cities, those representing different industries or having different kinds of merchandise for sale, are found together—such as shoe dealers, clothing shops, brass and metal workers, fruit, grain, meat and fish, dealers, etc. There are even sections devoted to the sale of second-hand shoes as well as second-hand clothes. Over the shop-doors are four characters in black or red, and hanging in front of them are boards or signs, painted or lacquered in black or red, with characters in gilt, containing some seductive invitation, high-sounding sentiment, sage aphorism, or extract from the classics. These swinging boards, suspended perpendicularly, give a brighter appearance to the long, low rows of otherwise dark and dingy-looking shops.

It is a characteristic of them all that their various industries, in all their various stages, are carried on before the public eye. The open front, as wide as the shop itself, exposes not only the manufactured product, but the process of manufacture. Here, for example, is a shoe shop. Around the sides are shelves bearing rows of completed shoes, while on the floor, on bench or table, every step of the process by which they are made is going forward. So of the furniture shops, where the chips and shavings fly in the midst of chairs and tables and cabinets exposed for sale. Brass workers and blacksmiths, stripped to the waist and grimy with dirt, pursue their noisy callings and fill the air with their din. The hulling of rice and cooking of meats and baking of cakes goes on before the eye of the passer, and the smoke of the latter, loaded with the odor of boiling fat, adds one more to the nauseous smells that greet his nose.

Prominent among the shops and industries are those connected with the superstitions and idolatry of the people. Here is a shop where one may see the entire process of making a god out of a block of wood or a lump of clay, till it emerges from the maker's hand, gilded and painted and curiously fashioned, to become in time the object of worship. In this shop alongside, or across the street, boys are stamping small sheets of paper for the ancestral worship, into representatives of copper cash, silver and gold coin, clothing, etc. In yet another men are building up light frames of bamboo to be covered with thin paper, in the shape of sedan chairs, articles of furniture, and sometimes miniature houses, to be burned at funerals or ancestral feasts.

Scattered among the other shops, more frequently perhaps than any others, are the cook shops, tobacco shops, eating houses and opium dens. The foreigner finds none of them attractive, though to the native they are sufficiently seductive. The opium dens differ from other shops in being partly enclosed, so as to hide the occupants generally from public sight. Over one of them is said to be this inscription: "May health and happiness rest on all who enter here!" The proprietor must have smiled ironically, or diabolically, when he put it up. There can be no denying that opium is the great curse of China—accepted at first unwillingly and under protest, but now adopted and its cultivation extending over a constantly widening field.

Right in the midst of this crowded city, and on streets filled with such sights, sounds and odors as I have feebly attempted to describe, are planted the two churches of Amoy. All these are precisely the same on Sunday as on any other day of the week. Added to them may be, and often are, the hideous music—fifes, horns, and beating of drums and gongs—and the snapping of firecrackers, with which idol processions and feasts are accompanied, with the shouts of the rabble which follow the processions. Through these the missionaries and native Christians must make their way, and carry on their worship in the midst of them. How difficult it must be to preserve the Sabbath decorum and the Sabbath spirit under such conditions, it is difficult for one who has not seen and felt them to conceive.

CHAPTER XXV.

THE AMOY CHURCHES.

AMOY, May 16

To continue the account of Amoy and its mission work: The first church, that of Sin-koi-a, occupies the building erected by Mr. Pohlman. Probably the first erected specially for Christian worship by Protestant missionaries in China, it is still a strong, substantial building of brick, and of size convenient for a considerable congregation. It was with a peculiar feeling of interest that I visited it the first time, and thought of the spirit of faith and prophecy which inspired him who built it. It must have required both to enable him to believe that it would one day be filled with willing worshippers of Him for whose name's sake he had gone forth. With what joy and holy satisfaction would he have seen (who shall say he did not see?) that church on the occasion of our second visit. It was a union communion service, in which pastors and people of the First and Second Churches were united. The male members of the two churches filled the body of the church down to the very doors. The space reserved for women, in the rear and at the sides of the pulpit, was equally well filled. Seldom has it been my privilege to attend a more interesting service, and never did I wish more fervently for the gift of tongues. The contrast was striking, indeed, between this quiet assembly, uniting in the simple but solemn service, and the thronged and busy streets through which we had come thither. Once in a while there came through the open windows the discordant sounds of an idol procession, once passing quite close to the church, and the report of strings of firecrackers, discharged probably in honor of some festive occasion. They broke on, but did not seriously disturb the stillness of the hour, or the prayers and praises that went up from grateful hearts, save as they suggested thoughts of pity for the great multitudes without, and desires and prayers for the speedier coming of that day when all the many tongues in all this broad land shall confess that Jesus Christ is Lord, to the glory of God the Father.

In the Second Church of Tek-chiu-ka, we first met the native brethren of Amoy in their assembly. This, also, was a union meeting of the two churches, and this church, too, was thronged with an attentive and evidently an interested congregation. The women especially were out in force and filled the space assigned them, disadvantageous as it is. The salutations of the churches in America and India were presented. Mention was made of the completion of fifty years of Gospel light and work since David Abeel first came, bringing the message of salvation. The pastors of both churches followed in brief addresses, and the whole congregation stood while they returned thanks for the work that had been done, and the missionaries who had lived among them, and expressed their desire that their greetings should be conveyed to the churches in America and in Japan.

Just as the service closed, an old woman was observed leaning over the screen that separates the woman's quarter from the men's, evidently laboring under considerable excitement, and desiring to be heard. We stopped to speak with her, and listened with great interest as she bore her testimony to the blessings she had received. For over forty years she had been a believer, and was now, at the age of eighty-two, rejoicing in the hope of the glory of God. It was not always so, she declared. For when the teachers first came she " hated the doctrine," and would not go near the place where it was taught. She hated and despised both those who taught and those who believed it. But when trouble came and her old gods failed her, the comforting words of the Gospel entered and possessed her heart. "It is nothing but the power of God," "the power of God," she repeated, with great emphasis. Her earnestness of speech and manner was very impressive, and the story she told a most striking illustration of God's saving power and grace.

The occasion of a second visit to this church was an elaborate feast given by the members of the two churches to all the missionaries at Amoy, as well as to the visitors, who, let it be said with becoming modesty, were the chief guests. In fact, the feast was given partly in their honor, and partly to commemorate the "Year of Jubilee." It was in true Chinese style, and extensive preparations had been made for it. The original invitation was given some days beforehand. On the morning of the day fixed, the pastor of the church called on the guests, presenting them with elaborate invitations on red paper and in Chinese character.

At the hour appointed we took boats and were landed very near the church. The building itself, its courts and the approaches, were thronged with people of all ages. A Chinese band struck up discordant strains as we entered, and continued to discourse at intervals during the evening—happily, in the outer court. Arrived at the entrance, we were met by the pastors and officers of the two churches, and conducted within with much ceremony of low bows, with clasped hands, bending almost to the ground. Leading the way and clearing a path for us through the crowd, which filled the women's apartment, the windows (even the skylights above) and all the passages, they ushered us in. The church was brilliantly decorated with banners, scrolls, lanterns and artificial flowers. Some of the hangings were of embroidered tapestry, very fine and evidently old. These, and a number of large lanterns, such as are used at marriages only, were loaned for the occasion. On one banner over the pulpit was inscribed in large Chinese characters, "Year of Jubilee," and on another at the opposite end, "East and West United." Six tables, each with eight chairs, were set, covering the floor of the men's portion of the church. One of these, the table of honor, was decked with artificial flowers, beautiful and elaborate, made of pith by one of the members of the church.

After a brief space for inspection and conversation, the complicated ceremony of seating the guests began. Two elders, dressed in full Mandarin costume, faced each other, representing, one, the hosts, and the other, each guest in turn. To one of these was handed the chop-sticks which were to be used by the guest. He received them in both hands, raised them to the level of his eyes and, holding them thus before him, bowed to the ground. Then rising, handed them over to be placed upon the table. The other, Mandarin-clad, with hands clasped before him, followed closely all these genuflexions. Similar bowings took place with a small glass of a peculiar sort of tea. The guest was then conducted to his seat. As there were forty-eight guests and this ceremony was repeated for each one, nearly an hour was thus consumed. Though the feast was to be in the true Chinese manner, yet a wide departure from custom was made in behalf of the ladies, two tables being specially set apart for them, and (wider departure still, if possible) a pastor's wife assigned to each to play the part of hostess. When all were seated, prayer was offered by the Rev. J. Macgowan, of the London Mission, and the feast began. Into the details it is hardly necessary to enter, as I have already described the dinner given to us by the Mandarin at Sio-khe. This closely resembled that, differing chiefly in the greater number of courses and peculiar dishes. Of courses there were twenty-one, beginning with edible bird's nests, and ending with pound cake and kisses of foreign make and style. Such toothsome dishes as sea-slugs, pig's tripe, etc., etc., were interspersed. After the fourteenth course a recess or intermission of five minutes was taken, when each guest was at liberty to get up, walk about and hold conversation with his fellows. When the last course was served the chief guest was privately notified that the end had come. His rising was the signal for the rest to rise, and all was over.

Yet not all. For soon one of the elders presented himself and, with a low bow and clasped hands, begged that the guests of the evening would not be offended by the want of politeness shown them; the people had sought to do us honor, but had been guilty of great lack of attention, and, in short, the whole entertainment had proved a miserable failure. According to Chinese etiquette this was the proper thing to do and say, albeit a sly twinkle in the speaker's eye, and an arrested smile on his artificially solemn countenance, gave token that, say what he might, they had done the thing up very creditably for themselves and very honorably for us. To this it was easy to reply—and truthful as easy—that we were delighted with our reception and the attention shown us, far beyond any desert of ours, and that we thanked them heartily for such an exhibition of their kindness.

Farewells were being spoken when the band put forth its utmost efforts, while a tremendous fusillade of giant crackers in the outer court made further speech impossible. The din was indescribable, and we were glad to escape after bidding an inaudible adieu to the many friends who had so exerted themselves in our behalf. That nothing might be wanting for our comfort, torches were provided, with which we were conducted through the dark and crooked streets to the boats. It was the finest feast and the most notable occasion in the history of the Church at Amoy.

LENG SOA AND PAGODA.

CHAPTER XXVI.

AMONG THE CHINESE CHRISTIANS.

AMOY, June 6

It has been thought desirable, and I myself have desired, to accept as many as possible of the invitations to visit the churches in the neighborhood of Amoy. The brethren have been so solicitous, and manifested so much kindly feeling, that it would have been ungracious to deny them. The first of these visits was made to Tong An, a large town some twenty-five miles north of Amoy, where the Mission are anxious that a station should be established, with two resident families and a hospital. The town itself is important, and the work there has had a remarkable development of late through the zeal and efficiency of Pastor Lim. But still greater importance attaches to it by reason of the large number of villages which dot the plains around it. Thither Mr. Rapalje accompanied me, acting as guide, interpreter and friend.

We boarded the Gospel Boat on a bright Saturday afternoon at two o'clock. The tide was favorable, and the breeze fair, though light. Toward evening it died away almost entirely, and our boat grounded on the shoals, which are of wide extent in all these waters. At the best, we could only hope to take the boat to Chiohjim, a small village about four miles short of Tong An. It had been arranged with the brethren that if we arrived before dark they would meet us with chairs and take us up the rest of the way overland. Should we arrive too late for this, we were to spend the night on the boat and go up early in the morning. By reason of the delays mentioned above, it was after nine and quite dark when, creeping slowly up the creek, we came to anchor just below Chioh-jim. A solitary boatman hailed us, and coming alongside declared that, just as he was finishing his supper, a large crowd had come down from Tong An, with chairs, music and fireworks, waiting for the " General Inspector of all the space under heaven !" whose arrival was anxiously looked for. Whether they were still there or not he could not say. He was sent back to see, and in half an hour returned with the chapel preacher from Tong An, who reported that most of the people had despaired of our coming and returned to the city, but chairs and burden-bearers were still there, with one or two other brethren.

Late as it was, we resolved to proceed. The moon had risen and lent no little light in the open country, while torches illuminated the dim streets of Chioh-jim and Tong An. A moonlight chair-ride of four miles through a strange country, and that country China, is an experience not soon to be forgotten. The roads, outside the village, which recent rain had made wet and slippery, were frequently nothing but narrow ridges dividing one rice field from another. A single misstep on the part of either bearer would have been sufficient to plunge us in the mud on either side, and make our own clothes abhor us (See Job 9:31). Happily no such accident befell, and no sound broke the stillness save the croaking of innumerable frogs, which make the rice field their abode, or the cry of the head chairman to his comrade in the rear. Stepping up or down, over an intersecting ditch or narrow bridge, turning to right or left, at each turn or obstruction, he uttered his note of warning, which was answered by his mate. These chair-bearers are a class by themselves—the very lowest, and are almost without exception opium smokers. Their work is hard and its effect upon the system very wearing, while their pay is comparatively small. The drug appears to be their only solace. So low are they regarded that no chair-bearer is allowed to enter the public examinations, though in this restriction they are joined with actors, barbers, constables and Buddhist priests! There could hardly be a more significant commentary on the estimate in which the last are held.

The ride had ceased to be novel and weird, and became wearisome before we passed through a low gate and entered the straggling suburbs of the city outside the wall. Our pathway led, with many turns and through streets reeking with mud, completely through the walled city to the opposite suburb. To our surprise, it being near midnight, many people were still on the streets. Little companies were gathered, at intervals, gazing on the weary, stupid theatrical shows that were in full blast. The food shops were generally open, semi-illuminated by flaring torches or sickly lamps. About half way through the city we were met by a band of musicians sent to meet us. They seemed to emerge, like spooks, out of the darkness, clad in flaming red coats, bearing pipes and horns of various shape and size, from which they expelled a prolonged and fearful discord of ear-splitting sounds. Confined within the narrow streets the din was, at times, almost deafening. Timid-looking women thrust their heads out of doorways as we passed, and belated boys ran alongside, curiously gazing at the strange procession. The effect was irresistibly ludicrous, yet one felt like apologizing for being even the innocent occasion of such a tumult at such an unconscionable hour of the night.

As we approached the church a crowd met us which completely filled the street. We made our way with difficulty to and into the courtyard, which was jammed with people, men and boys, in a compact mass. Here our chairs were set down and we emerged from our cramped quarters amid the wildest excitement. The pastor and elders of the church bowed low in hearty welcome and immediately conducted us up a flight of steps to an open verandah, where we could look down upon the crowd. One could have walked on their heads as on a pavement, so closely were they packed. Here chairs were placed for us, and our appearance was the signal for a deafening discharge of firecrackers of all sorts and sizes, eclipsing any and all the Fourth of Julys we had lived through from boyhood up; then followed fireworks of various, curious sorts, some of them scattering serpents among the crowd, which dodged and swayed and roared in ecstatic enjoyment. Firecrackers seem to be the Chinaman's delight. They are used on all occasions, even in worshipping the dead. One comes to think that heaven would hardly be complete to a Chinaman without them. A tall pole stood in the ground, whence depended frames of paper, united by a long fuse. At the touch of fire these developed into fish, serpents, a bird cage filled with fluttering, fiery birds, a turtle, and finally, a revolving parasol scattering flame. This exhibition over, we were invited to partake of a Chinese supper! The two pastors, dressed à la Mandarin, went punctiliously through all the appropriate ceremonial of invitation and placing us at the tables. But there are limits both to capacity and endurance, and so, on the ground of weariness and fulness, and also that the Sabbath had already begun, we begged to be excused. Being graciously informed that if we would but drink three cups of tea, the proprieties would be satisfied, we cheerfully accepted the alternative, excused ourselves and went to bed. But, for an hour or more, the sounds that entered the little upstairs bedrooms where we were struggling to sleep, informed us that the feast was carried out.

Sabbath morning dawned bright and clear. Before we had concluded our simple breakfast the people had begun to assemble from the town and surrounding villages. Specially curious ones climbed the stairs and stood gazing on us as we ate till they were courteously dismissed. The inner courtyard gradually filled up, and by nine o'clock, the hour for early service or "little worship," the church itself was full. This service is a sort of catechetical exercise upon the lessons for the day. The lesson is read, verse by verse, by members of the congregation, both old and young, and questions asked and comments made by the chapel preacher. At 10 o'clock came the regular service. The church by this time was crowded to repletion, many heathen mixing with the congregation and crowding the passages and doorways. A light partition separated the women from the men. Many heathen women were among them. From their position it was somewhat difficult to hear, and some talking and confusion among them was the result. The verandahs over the doorway and in the rear were full of people, looking and listening through open doors and windows. It was a satisfaction to know that the church is almost as well filled as this every Sunday. Blessed with an active, energetic and enterprising pastor, the church manifests an altogether new and vigorous life. The address of the Secretary was well received, being interpreted by Mr. Rapalje. At its conclusion Pastor Li, of the O-Kang Church, who has been working here for some weeks during the temporary absence of Pastor Lim, replied, thanking the churches in America for what they had done for the people of China, and extending the greetings and Christian salutations of the congregation to them and to the churches in Japan. The entire congregation arose and remained standing while he was speaking.

At the close of the service, while the people who had come from a distance were eating the simple fare they had brought with them, we took the opportunity of inspecting the church buildings.

A high wall shuts off the enclosure from the street, through which a door opens into an outer court. In one corner of this court is an immense banyan tree, with widespreading branches. A tree is a sacred object with the Chinese. Quite a tumult was created not long ago when it was proposed to cut off a branch of this tree which overhung and was injuring the buildings. On the inner side of this court is a two-story structure, the upper rooms of which are used by the missionaries when making their visits. Between these rooms is a covered verandah which looks both outward and inward on an inner and outer court. These courts are connected by a covered passage beneath this verandah. On the further side of the inner court stands the church, a substantial building of brick, of good size, but too small for the congregation. Within the enclosure are also a small schoolroom, a house for the pastor, and a kitchen for the use of the people on Sabbath. Here they prepare their tea and food during the intermission.

Passing behind the church we came upon an interesting picture. Miss M. E. Talmage had joined the congregation while service was in progress, having come over from another village. Here she stood beneath a spreading tree, surrounded by a throng of women, Christian and heathen, to whom, with the aid of a Scripture rollpicture, she was telling the Gospel story. Much of such work have the ladies of this mission done and are doing. It is hard, trying, often disappointing, but it has and cannot but have its rewards.

After the Sabbath-school service, which was held at 2 o'clock, embraced the entire congregation, young and old, and filled the church, we climbed the hill which overlooks the town. Directly below us it lay, with its thickly clustered houses and teeming population. Many literati have their homes here, as the numerous stone posts or pillars which mark their houses attest. They are as yet well nigh unapproachable, and their influence affects the attitude of the people of the city. A beautiful plain surrounds it, dotted all over with villages embowered in trees, and hemmed in on every side by mountains. It was not necessary to take the estimate of the good native brother who thought there were "ten thousand" villages in sight, to see and feel that here is a large population, in town and village, hundreds of thousands needing the Gospel, and who could be easily reached were a station to be planted here.

Descending from this "Mount of Vision" we turned our faces toward Chioh-jim. The two pastors, in Mandarin costume, accompanied us on horseback, and a goodly company on foot, to the outskirts of the town. There, just outside the gates, farewells were exchanged, whole-souled and hearty, they returning to their homes and we to Chioh-jim and the Gospel Boat, which gave us shelter for the night and brought us safely to Amoy in the early morning.

CHAPTER XXVII.

CHURCHES, TOWNS AND TEMPLES ON AMOY ISLAND.

Amoy, June 15

We expect to leave to-morrow by the S. S. "Belgic," which calls here on her way to Yokohama, for a cargo of tea. Detained for several weeks as we have been by the illness of my daughter, we shall not be sorry to leave. Yet we shall never forget the unwearied love and kindness shown us by all the dear friends here, nor cease to be grateful for the kind Providence that ordered our detention among them, and not among strangers. These weeks have given us, too, opportunities for seeing many things which would otherwise have been passed by, and to make full acquaintance with this climate. I have nothing good to say of it. Its humid heat is trying beyond expression. The air lacks all vitality, and exercise is labor indeed. They tell me it is better in the fall and winter. I sincerely hope it is. Indeed it must be, or life here would become, in time, almost unendurable.

It is a singular fact that Amoy, whence large quantities of China teas used to be exported, now sends little or none of these to the outside world. Indeed, I believe the cultivation of tea has almost, if not entirely, ceased in this region. But a large trade is done in Formosa tea, which ranks higher than the old teas and has, with the aid also of Ceylon and India, I suppose, driven them from the market. Steamers ply constantly between Amoy and Formosa. They are quite small, as large vessels cannot enter the harbors—or roadsteads—of that island. Their cargoes are discharged here, for larger vessels to carry to Europe and America. When, as now, the new crop comes in, the Pacific Mail and the Occidental and Oriental steamers call here and load up, in order to get the crop as quickly as possible to the markets which wait for it. The "China" came in on the 4th inst., on this errand, and carried away, as I was told, some 1,400 tons of the fragrant leaves. A similar cargo, though not so large, awaits the "Belgic."

Our delay enabled us to visit several more of the towns and churches in the neighborhood of Amoy. The Church of O-Kang, composed of the congregations of Kang-tau (or Creek-head) and Kio-tau (or Bridge-head) had been exceedingly desirous that I should visit them and partake of a feast in Chinese style. After former experiences I cannot say that this was an added inducement. But the earnestness of the brethren and the fact that much faithful labor had been expended on these places, decided me to accept their invitation. These towns are on Amoy island, Kang-tau being about six miles distant from Amoy and Kio-tau three miles beyond that. The journey was made in chairs, the only sort of vehicle known to or possible on the roads about Amoy. Much of one's comfort in this conveyance depends on the bearers. Some move quite easily, while others keep one constantly jerked and shaken. At the best it is not easy to keep from sliding forward in a heap. For this the feet and knees must be kept constantly braced, which becomes wearisome after a while. Unless one leans back, his head bobs back and forth like one of the curious nodding mandarins the Chinese make, and if he does lean back, it is likely to beat a perpetual tattoo on the head-rest behind him. Yet long journeys are made in these chairs, over rough roads and among mountains, as well as on the plains.

Our road led us directly through and around one side

of the city, skirting for some distance the base of the wall of the old city. Getting out at last into the open, we struck the high road—one of the widest (from two to five feet) and best that I have seen. It led by graveyards, wound among fields and climbed up and down over ditches and mounds. The graveyards about Amoy form some of the most singular objects to be seen. The graves are arranged side by side in close array, hundreds and thousands of them rounded over and covered with white plaster as hard as stone. When I first saw them, from a distance, they appeared like an immense flock of peculiarly large white sheep lying side by side and covering all the ground.

Leaving the city and its graves we passed through several villages, some of considerable size, each of which seemed to have its own industry and its peculiar smells. In one or more the entire population were apparently given over to the manufacture of vermicelli. The very air reeked with the odor of it. Boys were grinding rice for it in large stone mills, a thick milky looking fluid issuing from them and being caught in buckets. Men were lifting the thickened substance out of great tubs and spreading it on wicker hurdles, which others carried out and spread along the road and in the fields, leaving the stringy compound to dry in the sun. All these and other processes were going on in the open street, before almost every door. The only process not so done, and which I did not see at all, was that of drawing out the semi-fluid mass into the long strings which give the article its name. That seemed to be performed somewhere within the penetralia of the shops or houses. The sights were not appetizing, to say the least.

Other villages seemed to be exclusively devoted to the making of boxes in which to pack the vermicelli for shipment, as these, of all sorts and sizes, were piled up in the streets and before the doors. Large quantities of this article are shipped to the Straits Settlements, Singapore, Penang, etc., where the Chinese, many of them from Amoy, have largely congregated. Across the creek, also, a number of large villages were to be seen, nestling at the foot of hills. All, or nearly all, of these, with many others which we did not see, have been repeatedly visited by preachers of the Gospel, missionaries and natives, but as yet with small success.

About half way to Kang-tau we came upon a broad open space where two roads met. Here were standing thirteen large, handsomely carved memorial portals. These singular erections of stone somewhat resemble the torii, or gateways, which stand at the entrance to temples or temple grounds in Japan. They are designed to commemorate the virtues of distinguished dead, and are to be found everywhere, in the streets of cities, in villages and—as here—in the open country. Two heavy pillars support an entablature—all of granite—which projects beyond the pillars at either end. Above this a smaller horizontal block is supported by short columns. Many of them are rich in carving, and at the base of the pillars, on each side, have the favorite Chinese grotesque figure of a lion. These portals cannot be erected without the Emperor's permission, and numerous petitions for it are constantly presented. The imperial authorization is cut on the topmost stone. The grounds on which permission is sought, and the character of the persons commemorated, vary greatly. Virtuous women, widows, "girls who were betrothed and whose affianced husbands died before they were married and who refused to be married again"—(India would be full of such monuments if such a custom prevailed there)—men distinguished for piety or longevity, etc.

Our entrance into Kang-tau was much like that into Tong-an, with the exception that we made it at midday instead of midnight. There was the same—or a similar—band to escort, and waiting pastors, elders and people to receive us, with bursting firecrackers, large and small. For this, great preparations had been made. The church was profusely decorated with scrolls, banners and lanterns. The usual benches had all been removed from the centre, and two rows of chairs facing each other were set in the midst. Taking these chairs, with the pastor and elders, we were immediately served with bowls, each containing two hard-boiled eggs divested of their shells and swimming in water sweetened and colored red. With these were handed chop-sticks, by the aid of which we were expected to capture and dispose of these elusive eggs. This was a game requiring skill and patience, but crowned at length with success. Then followed cups of a peculiar kind of tea, the nature of which I could not determine; after these, cups of real tea, and then cups of coffee.

To us, thus fortified after our journey, it was intimated that the time for worship had arrived. The people crowded in and filled the church, and after singing and prayer there followed the usual address by the guest of the occasion, rendered into Chinese by Mr. Pitcher, and responded to by the pastor on behalf of the people. The good women of the congregation sat behind the pulpit, but were evidently much interested, and many came up to the friend from far with kindly greeting after the service was concluded.

Of the "feast" that followed, suffice it to say that it was—as nearly as might be—a counterpart of that given us by the united churches of Amoy, of which I have already spoken. The good people, determined not to be outdone, had ordered from the same caterer a precisely similar supper. It would undoubtedly have drawn itself out to the same length had it been permitted so to do. But as we had still three miles to go and another people to meet, we were obliged to cut it short. Amid the clatter of firecrackers we bade our kind hosts farewell, and started for Kio-tau. Some of them would not be left behind. About a dozen, on gaily caparisoned ponies with tinkling bells, accompanied us, and before us went the band! Three miles of discord indescribable—so dismal as to be positively jolly. So we survived it, and in an hour reached Kio-tau.

Here the whole village was agog. The way to the chapel was completely filled with a curious and expectant crowd, and the chapel itself packed to its utmost capacity. We found it a small, dingy—I had almost said discreditable—affair. The women were seated in a side room and could only see and hear through a large open window. My sympathies were so wrought upon that I ventured to tell them that, as the presence of a church in a town stood for the worship of the only true God, the honor of God was concerned in it, and that they should, for His sake as well as their own, try to get another and better one; that if they would do what they could, I would do what I could to help them. This, I understand, they have begun to do, and for aid to them the Mission has sent, or is sending a special plea. It is a worthy object, and a plea that ought to meet response from some large-hearted Christian in America.* The duties of hospitality were not neglected here, the serving of eggs and tea preceding the service. The attention was fixed while the service lasted, though most of the men present, and many of the women, were heathen. Here, too, as everywhere, grateful response was made, and recognition of

---

* This plea has been generously responded to by the Woman's Board, so fruitful of good deeds of the kind, to the great joy of missionaries and people.

the benefits received from the Church in America. Our home churches need not fear lest their labors and favors have been bestowed on ungrateful souls.

While idolatry is everywhere prevalent in China, yet the objects of worship are varied and numerous. The only worship that is *universal* is that of ancestors. Of this, one evidence is the ceremonies practiced at the graves at certain seasons of the year, of which I have already spoken. Another, and quite as impressive, is found in the ancestral temples. These are often of great size and elegance, built and maintained at large expense by some powerful and wealthy family or clan. The finest one that I have seen is in the neighborhood of our Second Church, of Tek Chiu Ka, in Amoy. It is a large stone building, or group of buildings, fronting a wide, open court, paved with stone, which faces the harbor. On the left of the court is a series of apartments, dining and bedrooms, handsomely furnished in true Chinese style, for the use of the families composing the clan when they visit the temple for worship or feasts. The temple itself is very handsome. The stonework of the facade is literally covered with carving, both delicate and grotesque. Panels illustrative of historical passages—presumably in the history of the family—containing figures of men, women and animals in high relief, and cut with the utmost minuteness of detail. Other panels with trees and birds perched upon the branches in various attitudes and standing out free from the mass of stone. It is a pity that such delicate work should be marred, as much of it is, by paint—the effect of which is to cheapen and disfigure. The large doors which open on the paved court are lacquered and decorated with gigantic figures of heroes in all colors.

Within, the great hall is elegantly finished. A high roof is supported by lofty columns, columns and roof beams in black lacquer, richly gilded, with gilded cornices exquisitely carved, banners and lanterns. At the farther side stands a cabinet, elegantly carved and gilded, in which are arranged in rows, shelf above shelf, the tablets for the dead. These also are carved and gilded. On either side of the cabinet stands a shrine in which an idol sits. The order and cleanliness throughout were perfect, indicating scrupulous care—quite an uncommon thing, and in marked contrast with a similar temple on Kolongsu. There the exterior court was dirty, and the large doorway in front lumbered up with boxes and baskets, masts and sails of boats and other rubbish. The inner court, too, was foul with dirt and lumber.

The amount expended on the temple first mentioned must have been great—$50,000 it was said, though probably not more than half so much. Its custodians seemed proud of it, and willing and eager to have it inspected. They showed us much courtesy, offering small cups of tea for our refreshment, and removing railings, etc., for the benefit of one of our party who wished to photograph the interior. On our way home we came upon a pitiful contrast with all this rich display of wealth and family pride—a small niche in a wall, crowded with the commonest sort of tablets. A pot of sand in front of them served to hold the sticks of incense which were burned before them. These were the two extremes. But they served to show the hold which this system of worship has upon the entire people—high and low, rich and poor, literati and ignorant vieing with one another in their devotion to the spirits of their ancestors. This is felt to be one of the greatest—if not the very greatest—hindrances to the Gospel and its reception by the people of China. Some, like Archdeacon Moule, have sought to find a sort of via media, by which certain supposably good elements, such as reverence for the dead and faith in the resurrection, might be recognized in solemn services at the grave on stated occasions. But the opinion of the native Christians, pastors and others, and of all the missionaries I have met, is emphatic, that no compromise is possible, that every trace of it must be abandoned by those who accept the Christian faith and name.

There are many other subjects and objects of interest connected with our visit and observations here of which I would gladly write. But it would be impossible to cover all the ground, and so, with this, and ready to depart on the morrow, I bring these letters from China to an end.

GRADUATES OF 1892.—FERRIS SEMINARY.

CHAPTER XXVIII.

WELCOME TO JAPAN AND FERRIS SEMINARY.

The "Belgic" brought us safely and smoothly over "sultry summer seas" to Yokohama on the 21st of June. The previous day we saw in the distance the shores of Kiu-shiu, which we were loth to pass, and still hope to visit. All the morning of the 21st we skirted the eastern shore of Nippon, vainly seeking and hoping for a glimpse from the sea of Fujiyama, "the peerless mountain." But dense masses of sea fog settling over the land hid it from our sight.

We reached our moorings in the capacious harbor of Yokohama early in the afternoon. Around us lay many large steamers, both naval and commercial, with innumerable smaller craft, bearing witness to the importance of this largest of the treaty ports of Japan, and to the volume of trade and commerce which centres here. Before us, the prosperous looking town, lying low along the water's edge, with its wide Bund and many large and creditable buildings, and back of it the Bluff, covered with foliage and dotted with buildings, dwelling houses, schools, hospitals, etc. Quite prominent among them all stands the "Ferris Seminary," conspicuous by reason of its size, its somewhat sombre color, and its windmill. We needed no one to point it out to us. Description and photograph had prepared us to recognize it, as we did, at once. Beautiful for situation, as well as for the work it does—of which I shall proceed to speak presently—it seemed to give us a home welcome from afar, as indeed it proved a home for many happy days. After a slight interval of waiting we were glad to see on an approaching steam launch, the familiar faces of Mr. Booth, Prof. Wyckoff and Mr. Pitcher, who had preceded us some ten days in his departure from Amoy. It need hardly be said that our greetings were most cordial, nor was it long before ourselves and our belongings were transferred to the launch, which conveyed us to the shore At the "Hatoba," or landing, we were met by Dr. Ver-. beck and Mr. Ballagh, and thus, surrounded by all the brethren of the Mission now on the field, we made our long-expected and long-deferred entry of Japan.

In the lower portions of the town, as seen at first, the stranger landing in Yokohama might be pardoned for fancying himself in some European port. The height, architecture and substantial character of the buildings, the signs upon the stores and warehouses, and the width and excellence of many of the streets, go far to justify the impression. This portion of the city is occupied by foreign merchants, and has been almost entirely rebuilt since 1866, the previous city having been largely destroyed by fire. The long lines of jinrikishas, however, and troops of Japanese, begin at once to dispel the illusion, and by the time one has passed through the foreign quarter, over the bridge, through the narrower streets thronged with natives, and among the humbler native shops, it has vanished altogether.

Seated in rikishas, with others following bearing our baggage, we climbed the steep ascent of the Bluff and soon reached the gate of the Ferris Seminary, No. 178. Here a delightful surprise awaited us. Drawn up within the gate, on either side, stood the pupils in long rows, their happy faces smiling on us a hearty greeting. Not less hearty and smiling was the welcome we received from Mrs. Booth and the other ladies who stood waiting at the door.

I may as well own, at the outset, to another surprise. Notwithstanding all that I had heard and known of the institution, I was not altogether prepared to see buildings of quite so important, not to say imposing, a character, or, to speak familiarly, so extensive a "plant." The original building had been once considerably enlarged, giving a capacity for one hundred pupils. When the more recent and extensive enlargement was planned, this accommodation was altogether insufficient. A light temporary Japanese structure, capable of accommodating twenty scholars, had been built, and yet many applicants had to be turned away for lack of room. It was in the day of greatest desire for female education, and education in Mission Schools. The tide of opinion set strongly in that direction. To meet the demand that then existed and which seemed likely to increase, the new buildings were erected. Two large buildings, one devoted to sleeping and dining-rooms, and one to recitation rooms, with a large hall for assemblies and public exercises, were erected—the latter known as "Van Schaick Hall."* That they are not now filled with scholars is no fault of the enthusiastic principal, nor of the school itself. Even before their completion that reaction or revulsion of popular feeling set in, the effects of which have been experienced by all the Mission Schools in Japan. For three years and more, though the number of schools has increased, the number of scholars, both boys and girls, has steadily diminished. Many causes, into which I will not enter, have conspired, doubtless, to bring about this result. Prominent among them is the anti-foreign feeling, which found its expression in the cry, "Japan for the Japanese." Along with this, and

---

* Aside from school purposes Van Schaick serves other excellent uses, the second services on the Sabbath and the midweek prayer meetings of both the foreign and native Union Church, as well as many other public assemblies, being held in it.

perhaps partly as its outgrowth, has been the policy of the government to discourage "private" schools, among which Mission Schools must be counted in distinction from Government schools. The intensity of this antiforeign feeling is believed by the most intelligent observers to be passing away. Whether the pendulum will swing in the opposite direction, and the former prosperity of the schools return, may be a question. Time will show. Let us hope so.

But there is no question, I certainly have none, of the excellence of the arrangements of Ferris Seminary, or of the work done in it. Our long detention in China prevented our reaching Japan in time to see the regular work of this and the other schools, and much of the Church work, in progress. But we were, happily, not too late to meet the pupils and teachers before their dispersion for the summer, and attend the closing exercises both of the Ferris Seminary and the Meiji Gakuin.

The scholars and native teachers of the former had prepared for us, entirely at their own suggestion and under their own direction, a delightful reception for the afternoon and evening of our arrival. Invited to visit Van Schaick Hall, we found them all assembled and the hall adorned with flowers, arranged in Japanese style, for our inspection and admiration. Thence we were led to one of the apartments, where the formal and elaborate tea-ceremonial was rehearsed for our benefit. It was impossible not to be charmed with the ease and grace of manner with which its intricacies were conducted. The hostess received her guests seated on the spotless floor. The attendant, with measured step and frequent kneelings and bowings, brought in, one after another and each separately, the furnace, the kettle, the canister, the cups, placing them on the floor before the hostess. Then, when filled, each cup was presented, with similar ceremony, to the guest, who received it with both hands and held it admiringly, scrutinizing both cup and contents before drinking. Though there were but three guests to be served, I judge the ceremony occupied nearly or quite an hour. Returning to the hall, we witnessed some interesting Japanese games. In the evening an address of welcome, in faultless English, was read by one of the Japanese teachers, in softest tones of a most winning voice. This was followed by songs and recitations, among them the singing of "Father, take my hand." It was a day long to be remembered.

On the evening of the 23d, we witnessed a series of calisthenic exercises, admirably executed by all the girls, in Van Schaick Hall. They wore the simple dresses provided by friends in America, which are much better adapted for such use than their own flowing robes. This, I was glad to notice, was their only departure from Japanese modes of dress or of living. Neither here nor in any of our schools in India or China, did I observe any effort to change the habits of the scholars in such matters—in other words, to Europeanize them. Their sleeping-rooms and beds, their dining-rooms and food and methods of cooking, and their dress, all conform to native models and ideas. Nor, so far as I could judge, have their manners suffered. It was quite gratifying to notice, in one of the daily papers of Yokohama, which spoke in terms of unqualified praise of the English Exhibition of Ferris Seminary, which occurred on the evening of the 24th, the admission that, while the scholars gave such evidence of judicious and skillful training in their studies, they had lost nothing of their simple native modesty and grace.

I wish I had time to speak as I would like of that English Exhibition and of the Japanese Commencement which took place on the evening of July 4th, each of them in the presence of full and apparently delighted audiences. The English papers and essays were well conceived and well delivered—the Japanese may have been just as good, and probably were, though I could not understand them. The exercises, both literary and musical, reflected very high credit on teachers and pupils It was my privilege to present, with a few words of counsel, their certificates to the members of the graduating class, and I am not ashamed to say that it gave me as much pleasure as almost anything I have ever done. But I desist, lest my account of this school should seem disproportioned, and I myself to have Ferris "on the brain." I must at least be allowed to add, that a more pleasing band of young Christian ladies it would be hard to find in Japan than the six or seven native teachers in this school, all of them its graduates, and illustrating the excellence of the work done in it. Their teachers and their friends at home may well regard them with gratitude and hope.

CHAPTER XXIX.

BY RAIL TO TOKYO AND THE MEIJI GAKUIN.

An untimely and unfortunate attack of fever, which seized me on the "Belgic" and continued with considerable force for several days after our arrival, has driven me to this delightful mountain retreat, after preventing me from enjoying many of the pleasant occasions and "functions" which had been kindly prepared. It was a satisfaction, however, after being compelled to decline many invitations, and being forbidden by medical advice to do any speaking, to be able to go up to Tokyo and attend the Commencement of the Meiji Gakuin.

This occurred on the 29th of June. Under the kindly conduct of Mr. Ballagh we went up by rail in the morning. This is the first railroad built in Japan. It was constructed by English engineers, in the very best and most expensive manner, the cost per mile far exceeding that of any other railroad in the Empire, of which there are now a goodly number. This line is eighteen miles in length and was completed in 1872. It has served as an object lesson to the Japanese engineers, to whom the construction of the other roads has, I believe, been exclusively confided. Leaving Yokohama from a fine and extensive station, it crosses an arm of the bay and passes through the old town of Kanagawa. In the early days Kanagawa far outranked in importance Yokohama, which was then only an inconsiderably fishing village. But it lay on the Tokaido, the great road running north and south between Tokyo and Kyoto, the two capitals of the Empire. Along this road throngs of people were constantly traveling. The Daimios with their bands of armed retainers, were passing to and fro. Frequent collisions took place between them and the foreigners, not unaccompanied with bloodshed. In fact, the spots were pointed out to us where such acts of violence were committed, and foreigners attacked and killed. To avoid their recurrence, ground for business and residence was assigned in Yokohama. This latter place has thriven greatly, far outstripping Kanagawa, which still retains, in great measure, its primitive simplicity. Its name alone, I believe, survives as a memorial of its designation as one of the open ports of the Empire, being still used in public documents. But the places are still pointed out where the early missionaries and consuls had their residence.

Hence to the capital the railroad runs along the shore of the Bay of Yedo or Tokyo, the Tokaido nearly parallel, between it and the sea. The day was bright and beautiful, the sunlight dancing and sparkling on the rippling surface of the bay, or lighting up the rich green of the rice fields which lay all along the road and stretched far away to the west, till the mountains shut in the view. Frequent temples, some of them of large size, were to be seen, standing on the level in the midst of gardens and groves, or picturesquely perched on the hillsides, half hidden among the trees, with ascending steps and the ubiquitous "torii" or gateways indicating the approach to a sacred shrine. The temple at Kawasaki, one of the towns through which we passed, is extremely popular, and at intervals is thronged by multitudes of worshippers. Just beyond the road crosses the broad bed of the Tamagawa or Rokugo river, which, rising in the distant mountains, here pours its tide, through a number of mouths, into the sea. The delta thus formed smiles with verdure. The fields are dotted with men and women, patiently toiling in mud and water above their ankles and beneath a burning sun, tending and weeding the growing rice. A few moments more and we are at Shinagawa, the most southerly station of Tokyo and just within the city limits. It is also the station nearest to the Meiji Gakuin. We found Prof. and Mrs. Wyckoff snugly domiciled in a native house, prettily placed on a swelling knoll and nestling among trees.

If the European or American of average height has not already been impressed by the general shortness of stature which prevails among the Japanese, he is likely to be forcibly reminded of it when he enters and takes up his temporary abode in a Japanese house. Its construction is peculiar. The rooms are separated not by immovable walls, but by sliding screens—the "Shoji"—which can be entirely removed at will—thus turning several rooms into one at pleasure. The ceilings of these rooms may be of reasonable and respectable height. But the permanent beams on which the upper edges of the shoji slide, are scarcely more than five feet or five and a half from the floor. As a consequence, frequent contact with them is apt to be the result to the six-footer as he moves about, until he learns to bow to circumstances and practice due humility. The experience is no doubt valuable, if somewhat dearly bought. The effect of the screens is to impart a light and airy character to the houses, which, in a warm climate, has its evident attractions. For colder climes and winters such as ours, or as are experienced in the northern or more elevated portions of Japan, something more substantial would seem to be desirable.

It was pleasant to meet, at Mrs. Wyckoff's table, Dr. and Mrs. Thompson, among the oldest Presbyterian missionaries in Japan, and the Rev. Mr. Vail, of the Am. Methodist Mission, with his wife, who, as Miss Witbeck, was once connected with our own Mission and the Ferris Seminary. The changes that had taken place in Japan since Dr. Thompson's arrival formed one of the subjects of conversation. They have indeed been marvellous in many ways—not the least in the growth of the Church of Christ and the spread of Christian truth. To see the evidences of them is something to be greatly grateful for. How much more to have been permitted not only to witness them from their beginnings, but to have had a share in bringing them about.

The Meiji Gakuin is the Christian College of Tokyo. It is supported by the Missions of the Am. Presbyterian Church (North) and the Reformed Church in America. It was formed by the union of the schools of these two Missions, that of the latter having been previously at Yokohama and of the former in Tokyo. Instruction is given by the members of both Missions, our own having been represented, until this last year, by Drs. Verbeck and Amerman, Prof. Wyckoff and Mr. Harris. The beginnings, at Yokohama, were very small. Yet from the little band of students of English gathered by Dr. S. R. Brown, have come some of the ablest and most trusted preachers of the Church of Christ. To this college, and the kindred institution of our German Reformed brethren at Sendai, which we hope to visit, this church must chiefly look for its supply of educated pastors and preachers in the future for the northern and central portions of Japan. Its importance to the rising Church, therefore, can hardly be overestimated, nor the value of the work it is accomplishing.

The exercises of Commencement week were ushered in by the Annual Sermon, preached by the President, the Rev. Kajinosuke Ibuka, on Sunday evening. This was followed on Monday evening by the Junior Oratorical Contest, and on Tuesday evening by the Ninth Anniversary of the Literary Society, at which a varied entertainment was presented. All these, together with receptions of the missionaries in Tokyo and of the native pastors, which had been kindly prepared for us, I was reluctantly, but imperatively, obliged to forego. It was with the greater pleasure, therefore, that I found myself able to attend the Commencement exercises on Wednesday afternoon. These were held in the large chapel or assembly room in Sandham Hall, which was comfortably filled with students and friends of the institution. On the platform President Ibuka conducted the exercises with dignity and grace. At his left was seated the venerable Dr. Hepburn, the preceding President, who has been privileged of God to see fifty years of missionary service, at first in China and since 1859 in Japan. Between them your correspondent was assigned a place. The programme varied materially from that ordinarily in use on such occasions. None of the students then graduating made speeches, the only formal address being delivered in Japanese by one of the professors in the Imperial University. Diplomas were given to seventeen graduates from the academical and from the theological departments. An address had been assigned to me on the programme, from which I felt compelled to beg excuse. But when, in graceful sentences, President Ibuka expressed the sense of indebtedness of the institution and of the Church of Christ to the Reformed Church and her missionaries for the long continued and lively interest manifested in their welfare, it was impossible to sit still. On trembling limbs, and with a few broken but hearty sentences, it was a satisfaction not to be declined to give utterance to the pleasure I felt in such an occasion, and to earnest wishes for the continued prosperity of this Christian school.

In the evening the alumni had their annual dinner at

a restaurant in Shiba, one of the park-like districts of Tokyo. The association is of rather recent formation, but is doing good in cementing ties of friendship and promoting a lively interest in the welfare of Alma Mater. There we met Professors Knox, Imbrie, McAuley and John Ballagh, of the Presbyterian Mission, and Prof. Wyckoff of our own, beside President Ibuka and Profs. Ishimoto and Sugimura. A feeling of good fellowship seemed to prevail, and but for the "unknown tongue," one might have fancied himself among the alumni of one of our own younger colleges. That several of the speeches were in English helped the illusion.

The following morning we visited the college grounds and buildings. The situation in one of the outer quarters of the capital, less thickly settled, seems well chosen. The campus, a considerable parallelogram, lies as a table at the summit of a gentle acclivity. One side is flanked by four dwellings, the homes of as many professors. On the opposite side stands Sandham Hall, a fine building, the gift of Mrs. Sandham, of New York, devoted to recitation rooms and chapel, well arranged and adapted to the uses for which it was given. Next to it stands a noble library building of brick, containing also some lecture rooms—the gift of friends in America. Hepburn and Harris Halls, across one end of the campus, furnish sleeping and dining rooms for the students. The view from the cupola of Hepburn Hall is beautiful and commanding. Such is the wealth of foliage that one finds it difficult to fancy himself within the limits of one of the largest cities in the world. While other buildings may be desirable, and some are needed, I was, nevertheless, surprised and gratified to see so young an institution so well provided for present needs. The great want at present, as the trustees feel, is an endowment fund on which the college may rely for the maintenance and extension of its proper work. Looking to the future, and to its important relations to the growth of the Church of Christ, and regarding the material provision already made, I could not and cannot repress the wish that some one or more might be found to do for it what Christopher Robert did for the college on the Bosphorus which bears his name, or William E. Dodge and others for the Syrian College at Beirut. Neither of them, it seems to me, has brighter prospects for usefulness than this.

CHAPTER XXX.

BEAUTIFUL NIKKO AND THENCE TO SENDAI.

"He who has not seen Nikko cannot say kekko," ("beautiful!"). So runs the Japanese legend. And, indeed, it is not far out of the way. For beautiful it is, exceedingly. The Japanese are intense lovers of nature and keenly appreciate its varied beauties and glories. The various flower seasons—the cherry blossom, the iris, the wisteria, the lotus, the chrysanthemum—are seasons of great popular enjoyment. The parks and groves and gardens where these flowers abound in greatest profusion and glory, are the resorts of admiring multitudes. So, too, are the spots which the national taste has pronounced pre-eminent for beauty. When so much beauty is to be found everywhere, choice is not easy, and tastes will differ. But few, I imagine, would find fault with the judgment that exalts Nikko in the popular esteem. Beauties of art combine with those of nature to render it attractive. At an elevation of two thousand feet, seated among mountains clothed from foot to summit in living green—some with luxuriant forests, and some with no less luxuriant grass and herbage, it has a queenly throne. A noble mountain stream pours its perpetual torrent at its feet. Into deep mountain chasms numerous waterfalls leap—twenty or thirty of them, it is said, within a radius of fifteen miles. The air is pure and bracing, in marked contrast, at this season, with that in Yokohama and Tokyo and the plains below. The one great drawback, indeed the only one so far as I know, is the abundance of rain that falls here at all seasons, rendering somewhat inappropriate, one might think, the title given to the range, "Nikko-san,"—"mountains of the sun's brightness." Our own experience in this regard has been supremely fortunate, the sun shining clear by day, and the moon by night, for five days out of six. But friends of ours, who came earlier and spent a week, saw nothing of the "brightness," being enveloped during the whole time of their stay in clouds and rain.

Were I writing purely descriptive letters, as I am not, I might have much to say of those six glorious days, and of the many and varied objects of interest to be seen here and in this neighborhood—of the long avenue of stately and solemn cryptomerias, twenty-eight miles in length, by which it used to be approached from Utsunomiya before the railroad superseded it; of the sacred bridge, gorgeous in red and gilt, which spans the river just above the town, kept locked and barred so that none may pass over it but the "immortals," gods and the royal family, descendants of the gods; of the long row of stone Buddhas, stained by innumerable storms, and gray with the accumulated moss of many generations, which, to the number of a hundred or more, sit in silence on the right bank of the river, a mile or so above the bridge, dreamily contemplating the troops of visitors, the brawling river, and the hills beyond; or of the magnificent temples, mortuary memorials of the early Shoguns Ieyasu and Iyemitsu, the former the founder of the Tokugawa dynasty and of Yedo, now Tokyo, the latter the third in the succession. Wonderful in construction, in the wealth and artistic skill lavished upon them, these temples are no less wonderful for the remarkable state of preservation in which the visitor of to-day finds them, or for their setting in groves of cryptomerias, magnificent in size, height and straightness, but somewhat oppressive in their sombre density of shade. A massive stone stairway with stone balustrade, seeming as true and firmly set as when they were first placed, covered with moss and dripping with moisture, conducts, by more than 200 steps, to the tomb of Ieyasu, which surmounts and looks down upon the temple. But of none of these objects need I speak, so fully have they been exploited in the many books upon Japan which are easily accessible by every reader.

These temples have a somewhat peculiar interest for the Christian tourist, since it was under Ieyasu that the persecution of the early Christians began, a work of fire and sword completed by Iyemitsu, when the "corrupt sect" was believed to be exterminated, and those edicts were set up everywhere throughout the empire, on public tablets, which, until a few years ago, denounced "the evil sect called Christian" as "strictly prohibited," and promised rewards to those who should inform against persons suspected of belonging to it. One could hardly help wondering, if their spirits may be supposed to be cognizant of what is now transpiring in Japan, how these great patriots and persecutors regard the re-entrance of the doctrine they sought so vigorously to suppress and stamp out forever, the multitudes of their own people who have received it, and especially the troops of Christians from outside lands who visit their tombs, and penetrate to the inner chambers of their temples.

From Nikko we took an early start for Sendai and Morioka under the careful guidance of our good Dr. Verbeck. No man, probably, knows Japan and the Japanese better than he. And he is the one foreigner in all Japan who can live and travel wherever he pleases. Taking the train for Utsunomiya, we there changed cars for Sendai, 150 miles further North, and 215 miles from Tokyo. The road lay through a beautiful region, for the most part highly cultivated—the ubiquitous rice fields stretching away on either hand, and the summits of the

Nikko and other ranges visible on the West. Numerous pretty villages and larger towns lie along the road, and it was a surprise and pleasure to notice the schoolhouses everywhere. In many places—most of them, in fact—they were the largest and best buildings to be seen. One cannot but be impressed by the energy and intelligence which the government has shown in the establishment and development of its educational system. Repeated changes have been made as experience has shown their necessity, since the beginning of 1868. The present system starts with the kindergarten, of which there are ninety, and culminates in the Imperial University in Tokyo, with its departments of Law, Medicine, Engineering, Literature and Science. Between these extremes are the elementary or primary schools, the ordinary middle schools, the higher middle or colleges, and the normal schools. The pupils in all these schools number about three and a half millions. Beside these, not to speak of the various mission schools, there are numerous private schools, some of which, like that of Mr. Fukuzawa in Tokyo, the Keio Gijiku, are of great size and a high grade. While, with all this provision and the aid, I believe, of a compulsory education law, less than half the school population is yet at school, there still seems good reason to hope that the purpose expressed in an early imperial edict may one day be realized: "That education shall be so diffused that there may not be a village with an ignorant family nor a family with an ignorant member." Happy the land where that comes to pass.

The Japanese railroad is not noted for speed, and nine hours is a long time to consume in a journey of 150 miles. But the fine and extensive views of hills, mountains, rivers, valleys and plains opening in constant succession on either hand, the throngs of people entering and leaving the cars, and the novel scenes in the towns through which we passed, to say nothing of the pleasure of delightful companionship, made the way seem short. We reached Sendai in the cool of the evening, after an exceedingly hot day. Here we were met by the Revs. Oshikawa, Fuju and others, connected with the Mission of our German Reformed brethren, with the most cordial welcome, and conducted to the hospitable home of the Misses Poorbaugh. Before we were allowed to leave the station, however, our passports were demanded and carefully examined by members of the omnipresent police. Perhaps no country in the world is more thoroughly policed than Japan. Through all the country districts they are to be seen, as well as in the cities and towns, patrolling, either mounted or on foot, and guarding the smallest railway stations as carefully as the most important. It is part of their business to arrest the luckless or careless foreigner who may be found outside the treaty limits without a passport, and conduct him with all safety and expedition to the capital. Fortunately for us we were provided with the proper papers, and so escaped their hands.

Sendai is a considerable town of 70,000 inhabitants, and the capital of the province of Rikuzen. One of the northern Daimios formerly had his castle here. The castle, partly destroyed during the revolution in 1868, is now used for military barracks. The military governor of the N. E. provinces has his official residence here. The streets are broad, and many of them lined with inviting shops. Among the ordinarily low Japanese houses there are a good number of buildings, both public and private, in European style. Its special interest for us lay in the fact that the Japan Mission of the German Reformed Church has its central station here. Unfortunately, owing to the lateness of our visit, the members of the Mission were all absent. But a cordial note of welcome placed the house of the ladies at our disposal, and two gentle Japanese maidens waited to care for us and do us honor. The native brethren were also assiduous in their kind attentions.

The mission compound encloses the residences of the missionaries and the girls' boarding-school, of which more anon. The tidings of Dr. Verbeck's coming had preceded us, and notice had been given that a meeting would be held in the evening, at which he would speak. So, after supper, we sallied forth to the church, at no great distance, and on one of the main streets of the town. It was interesting to learn that the church building had once been a Buddhist temple. Its revenues had fallen off, and the priests, poor and discouraged, had sold it for a comparatively low price. Later they had repented, and sought to buy it back at a considerable advance, but to no purpose. A Christian church it now is and is likely to remain, unless another and better should be built on the same site. With every trace of idolatry removed, a raised platform and desk, and seats for the audience, it served its present purpose well. We found it nearly filled. The service, under the conduct of Mr. Oshikawa, began with singing, with the aid of an American organ. Dr. Verbeck gave a short and animated address. The writer was then introduced, with a few sentences appreciative of the work done by the Reformed (Dutch) Church through its missionaries in Japan, and responded briefly, thus making his first address to an audience in Japan. It was an experience not to be forgotten—the place, transformed to Christian uses from the worship of idols—the audience, partly composed of Christians and partly of curious or inquiring heathen, and a large proportion of them young—everything, in short, tended to make it profoundly interesting and impressive.

The German Reformed Church is represented in Sendai

by the Rev. Messrs. Hoey, Moore and Schneder, and Misses E. F. and L. R. Poorbaugh. They have two flourishing educational institutions under their care. Of these, the girls' boarding-school, as I have said, stands in the mission compound. It is a large frame building, containing chapel and recitation rooms, and sleeping and dining-rooms in Japanese style for the pupils. The building cost 7,000 yen, about $5,000 in gold, and is well adapted to its designed uses. It can accommodate some fifty scholars, and had forty-four upon its roll last year. Though the summer vacation had commenced, several of the scholars remained in the school, and their bright, happy faces were pleasant to look upon. Their voices too, sounded sweetly as, raised in songs of praise, they came across to us in the early morning. After going through the building, and exchanging greetings with the scholars, we went accompanied by Mr. Oshikawa, to visit the other and larger institution, of which he is the head.

The Tohoku Gakuin, or Northeastern Institute, is the school for boys and young men. It possesses a large and handsome building of brick, of imposing external appearance, and admirably fitted up within. It was built at a cost of about 10,000 yen, $7,000 in gold, and was opened for use in September 1891. The number of students this year is 120, divided among three departments, preparatory, academic and theological. The last with twelve students, is again divided into two departments, Japanese, with seven students, and English, with five. Two foreign teachers (missionaries) and eight Japanese teachers are employed. The beginnings of a good library are also there. It is an institution in which our German brethren may well take great satisfaction. The ground on which it stands immediately adjoins that belonging to the church already mentioned, and these together afford room for other buildings as they may be needed.

The tower commands a fine view of the city and surrounding country.

The city is the centre of a populous district. The Mission has four preaching places within the town, together with half a dozen in Miyagi and three in Yamagata Kens. Much good and substantial work has been done. The city church, under the pastorate of the Rev. I. Miura, has a membership of 362. It was begun as an independent church, but has been for some years connected with the Mission. How large the membership is outside the city I do not know. A fine field, with abundant promise, and good facilities for working it, are in the hands of our German brethren. May the Lord give them abundant success.

CHAPTER XXXI.

MATSUSHIMA AND MORIOKA.

OUR time at Sendai being limited, we were unable to see anything of the work of the American Board, which has a station here. This we regretted the less as Dr. DeForest was absent. One incident of our stay we must not forget. On the evening of our arrival we were waited upon by a Mr. Sugeto, who, having heard of our coming, had travelled all the way from Sapporo in the Hokkaido to meet us and to plead that missionaries might be sent to that island. The Hokkaido, or "Circuit of the Northern Sea," is the island formerly called Yezo. On it is Hakodate, one of the ports first opened to foreign trade by treaties with Japan. It lies north of the main island, has a colder climate, a harsher soil and a less cultivated people. Here, too, the Ainu, the remnant of the aborigines of Japan, are found. Of late years efforts have been made to induce settlement by emigrants from other parts of Japan, and with considerable success. At Sapporo an agricultural station was established, and for some years carried on by General Capron and a number of American assistants. This experiment was afterward abandoned as too costly, but a respectable agricultural school or college is still maintained by government. It was the cause of the emigrants, as well as of the scattered inhabitants of the island, that Bro. Sugeto came to plead, and plead it he did most earnestly, dwelling upon the wide opening and the condition of the people, "as sheep without a shepherd." This was but one of many similar appeals to which we have listened from time to time on this tour, of which we could not but feel and admit the force, and yet to which we were unable to give affirmative or even encouraging response. Alas for the necessity of silence under such circumstances! It was impossible to repress the secret wish that our German brethren, so firmly planted and so successful in their work at Sendai, might be moved to extend their operations by sending missionaries to the Hakkaido. Their situation so far north, would be favorable for such a movement.

We left Sendai in the early afternoon of an extremely hot day, July 12th, *en route* for Morioka, 113 miles further north—328 miles from Tokyo—but stopping over night at Matsushima. These places all lie on the great Northern Railway, which has been recently completed to Aomori, a small but rapidly growing seaport, about 500 miles from Tokyo and near the extreme northern end of the great island of Nippon. So rapid has been the growth of Aomori, and so great the demand for houses, that the preacher stationed there, the Rev. Mr. Maki, has found it impossible to secure a suitable place for residence and preaching place. Matsushima is the title given to an archipelago of islands mostly quite small and said to be more than 800 in number, lying in and off the Bay of Sendai. It is one of the *San-kei*, or "Three most beautiful Scenes" of Japan, and seems to be well worthy of its long established reputation. I say "seems" advisedly, because we were so unfortunate as to have the larger view cut off by fog rolling in from the sea, and settling down over the outer islands. What we did see, however, was sufficient to make us well content. The village of Matsushima is about two miles and a half distant from the railway station of that name, and is directly on the shore of the bay. We made the distance in rikishas. Just before reaching the village we left our vehicles and climbed a hill which overhung the road and overlooked the sea. A well-defined path led up to a small shrine upon the summit. Thence there spread out before us a scene of peculiar beauty—islands of all sizes clustered together, covered with pines, some of dense and vigorous growth, and not a few with but a single tree or two, or three, and seeming scarcely large enough to support even them. Their walls, of a soft volcanic rock, rose abruptly from the water, like the sides of a ship, and gave to the group the appearance of a verdant fleet that had grounded or come to anchor in the bay, with tall trunks for masts and wide-spreading branches for their sails. With the movement of the fog before the wind other islands would appear for a moment, only to be speedily enveloped and hid from sight.

Descending from the hilltop, and making our way to the village, we took up our quarters for the night at a native inn, the Shio-to-quan. This was our first experience of such entertainment, though destined not to be the last. This house was neat and airy, with open windows and balcony, perched on a little knoll and looking off upon the water and the islands. We called it "The House of the Seven Gables," from its quaint appearance. Whether that was the meaning of its name I do not know, though it might easily have been. The first thing for an arriving guest to do is not to register his name, but to take off his shoes. This is the indispensable condition of entrance to a true Japanese house, as of the temples and many of the places for Christian worship. The reason is at once apparent, for the floors are covered with thick matting, kept scrupulously clean, on which the people sit without intervention of chair or stool. Aside from the desire for cleanliness, the sharp heels of foreign shoes would soon make havoc of the mats.

The proprietor—or his representative—and the waitresses kneel at the entrance and prostrate themselves before the coming guest. Mounting the stairs, two large rooms, from which the shoji, or dividing screens, had been removed, were placed at our disposal, our articles of luggage variously bestowed, and almost as soon as we were seated on the spotless floor, tea was brought in. Refreshed with tea and rest, we went out as the day grew cooler and visited several of the islands connected with the mainland by bridges. Every island in the entire group is said to have its name. Some of them—as had one of those we visited—have shrines and temples on them and others dwelling houses. On one the rocky edge had been excavated so as to form a continuous series of cavernous niches, in many of which still stood images of the gods. Some of these images were in fairly good preservation, some worn and mutilated, while many had disappeared altogether, leaving their places vacant. The rock itself seemed to be disintegrating and likely, at some distant period, to disappear. A Tokyo merchant had built a summer cottage on this island—a beautiful spot indeed. In passing through the village we noticed many dark caverns under overhanging rocks, the rocks themselves covered thick with vines, while immense trees, rooted in the crevices, had sent other roots downward, clinging to the surface, to seek nourishment from the ground below.

A true Japanese dinner was served us in the evening, in lacquered trays set before each as we were seated on the floor. The food consisted chiefly of fish—cooked in different ways—soup, a few other vegetables and a bowl of rice—all to be eaten with chop-sticks. The people who use these implements far outnumber those who employ knives and forks, and the expedition with which a good meal can be eaten with their aid by an expert is simply marvellous. Where every smallest child is such an expert, the almost helpless foreigner feels his inferiority. With the introduction of lights the ubiquitous mosquito makes his already suspected presence more distinctly felt. No country enjoys a monopoly of these "birds of prey." To ward them off and make sleep possible, a huge net is brought in and suspended from the four corners of the room. Beneath its spreading folds four beds are spread upon the floor—layer upon layer of thickly wadded quilts, cotton and silk—with one for covering. Stretched upon these and sheltered by the net we slept and were refreshed, unmindful of mosquitoes and forgetful of Matsushima and its charms.

An early call—before sunrise the next morning—roused us to begin the journey of the day. After a hasty cup of tea we took the waiting jinrikishas again and sought the station. The fog still lingered and the early morning air was chill. Climbing a steep hill some distance beyond the village, we turned seaward and saw our last of Matsushima. Our vision of it had been limited, yet we had seen much to admire. With the aid of a little imagination it was easy to understand the charms it possesses for the nature-loving Japanese. One of their poets, we were told, was so impressed by them that he gave expression to his feelings in a poem. According to the rules of the Japanese *Ars poetica*, a poem may consist of only a few syllables, each, however, possessed of poetic force and meaning. The poem to which I have referred read thus:

> "Matsushima yah!
> Tada (only) Matsushima yah!
> Ah! Matsushima."

Morioka is the most northerly station occupied by any

of the Missions connected with the "Church of Christ in Japan." The Rev. E. Rothesay Miller and Mrs. Miller, of our own Mission, removed thither from Tokyo in 1888, and have since resided there continuously until June, 1892. Mr. Miller's attention had been called to it some years before, while on a tour in the north, as a desirable point at which to begin and from which to superintend evangelistic work. A considerable company of believers has been gathered, numbering last year sixty-two. Work has also been done in neighboring towns, and very interesting services have long been held in the prison with encouraging effect. Mr. Miller has been assisted by the Rev. Mr. Miura, of the native Church. Here also Mrs. Miller has done a good work among the women, besides continuing the preparation and publication of the monthly periodical established by her, the *Yorokobe no-otudzuri*, or Glad Tidings. This excellent paper has reached a circulation of 3,500 copies, and is taken in nearly every province of the Empire. When Miss Leila Winn returned to Japan in 1891, she was transferred from the Ferris Seminary to Morioka, to engage directly in evangelistic work among the women. It was my hope to be able to visit Mr. and Mrs. Miller in their own home, and under their conduct to see the work that has developed in this interesting field. But our protracted delays by the way prevented this, and they were already in America on well-earned furlough when we turned our steps westward. Our welcome was cordial and hearty notwithstanding, and we found awaiting us at the station on our arrival Miss Winn, the Rev. Mr. Pierson, of the Presbyterian Mission, temporarily stationed there, Mr. Miura, O Hira San, Miss Winn's assistant from the Ferris Seminary, and other Japanese friends. Notwithstanding the higher latitude, the sun was scorching, and we were glad to escape from it into the shelter of Mr. Miller's comfortable home.

On the outskirts of the town, among trees and gardens, the house is a composite of Japanese and American ideas and construction, combining the light and airiness of the former, with not a little of the comfort and solidity of the latter. A veritable home-garden, with familiar plants and vegetables in flourishing condition, added to its attractions. The town is beautifully situated between two ranges of mountains, and not far distant rises the symmetrical summit of Iwate San, the northern Fuji. It is also a place of considerable importance, both for trade and as the possessor of the Court House, the High School, and the official residence of the principal officers of the Prefecture. In former times a daimio had his castle here. The walled enclosure still remains, surrounded by a moat, now dry, and overshadowed by noble cryptomerias. Of the castle itself, no vestige now remains. At least we found none, as we clambered over the walls and through the rank vegetation in the afternoon. Just so completely has the old-time feudal system disappeared from Japan.

More interesting far than any such objects was the meeting in the evening, at the house of Mr. Miura, where we met the native brethren, and spoke a few words to them, in company with Dr. Verbeck, Mr. Miura and Mr. Maki, of Aomori. It was pleasant to see so many bright, intelligent-looking young men in the company. The next day Miss Winn had her class of women gathered at her house for prayer. As we sat in the room above, it was sweet to hear the sounds of praise, and the low murmur of voices tuned to prayer that came to us, and then to be invited down to take these sisters by the hand and look into their faces even for a moment.

Work in this region might be much extended were it

not for the passport system of which I have already spoken. Miss Winn goes to Hanamaki, where she has a class of women, as Mrs. Miller did, but must return before night. The same restriction applies to Mr. Pierson's movements. Neither he nor Miss Winn could obtain a passport permitting them to reside at Morioka were they not engaged in teaching in one or other of the Japanese schools here. The same is true of all foreign residents in interior towns. By so much as the restriction is rigidly enforced is the possibility of missionary labors circumscribed. It is no wonder that missionaries generally long for the day when, by a revision of existing treaties, this disability may be removed.

At Morioka our little party separated. Mr. Booth with one companion went north to the Hokkaido. Miss Deyo remained to spend a few weeks with Miss Winn, while we, my daughter and myself, returned with Dr. Verbeck to Tokyo. Of this great and peculiar city I shall hope to have something to say in my next letter.

CHAPTER XXXII.

GLIMPSES OF TOKYO.

WE have really seen so little of Tokyo that I am quite reluctant to speak of it at all. It is impossible to get any adequate or even clear idea of such a city in four or five days, which, split into two nearly equal portions, was all we had to give it. One of these we spent as the guests of Prof. and Mrs. Wyckoff in their cozy Japanese house at Shinagawa, on the occasion of the Meiji Gakuin Commencement. The other and later, in Tsukiji, or the Foreign Concession, as guests of Dr. and Miss Verbeck. The distance between these two sections of the city, some four and a half or five miles, gives one some faint conception of its extent and peculiar characteristics.

It is a city of many quarters, and seems to have grown by agglomeration—the gradual absorption of scattered and outlying villages or districts, until it covers an irregular space of about ten miles square. Some of these quarters are still quite rural and even park-like—large and beautiful parks, shaded by noble trees being included in them—while in others the houses are as thickly compacted, though with broader streets, as in any city in China. In olden times it was a simple fishing village, and bore the name of Yedo. As such it was known to the Western world until recent years. The first Shogun, Ieyasu, made it his residence in the opening years of the seventeenth century, and since that time, and up to the Revolution of 1868, it has been the capital of the Shogunate, or military power, the Mikado or real Emperor having his capital at Kyoto. When, by the Revolution, he was restored to actual power, and began to exercise the legitimate supremacy of which he had been so long deprived, he came to Yedo, and the name of the city was changed to Tokyo, or the "Eastern Capital." Its present population is about a million and a quarter.

Tsukiji, or the Foreign Concession, is the quarter assigned for the residence of foreigners. Such a quarter is assigned for this purpose in all the open ports, and foreigners are not permitted to live outside of them unless they are employed for some purpose, educational or other, by natives of the country, or by the government. The space occupied is comparatively small, and is mostly taken up by the churches, schools and residences of the missionaries of the various bodies represented in the capital. Yet not all of these are here by any means, the Methodist Episcopal Church (North) of the United States having their college and theological school at Aoyama, and the Meiji Gakuin of the Presbyterian and Reformed Churches being at Shinagawa, each at a distance of several miles from Tsukiji and from each other. The Graham Female Seminary of the Presbyterian Mission is also located in another quarter of the city, and there may be others beside. Specially prominent among the buildings of the Foreign Concession is the fine group erected —and hardly completed at the time of our visit—by the Mission of the Episcopal Church in the United States. This Mission is largely indebted, for its strength and success, to the personal character and devotion of the venerable Bishop Williams, who was one of the first missionaries to Japan, residing during the early years, from 1859, at Nagasaki.

None of the schools, unfortunately, were in session at this season, and we were obliged to be content with viewing the outside. The American Legation used to be domiciled in Tsukiji. The building occupied by it is still one of the most conspicuous in the settlement, is finely situated on the Bund, looking off upon the water and catching the evening breeze, and is now the Club Hotel, where we were most hospitably and comfortably entertained.

Prominent among the objects of special interest in Tokyo are its magnificent parks of Shiba and Ueno. We visited the former early in July. Here six of the Tokugawa Shoguns lie buried, in mortuary temples whose display of gold and lacquer work, architectural and artistic elaboration and adornment, at first dazzle and bewilder and at last—shall it be confessed ?—confound and weary the beholder. As one passes through the various ornamented gateways, and the courts lined with curiously adorned and colored buildings, and long rows of lanterns in stone and bronze and shadowed by overarching trees ; as, with shoes removed and the proper (and very moderate) fee for entrance paid, he treads on lacquered floors and looks upon tombs and walls and ceilings lacquered and gilded and rich in carving and other decorations in the highest style of art known to Japan, he is oppressed with a sense of richness beyond expression—his ejaculations of wonder and admiration seem enfeebled, language impoverished, and his vocabulary to need enlargement with each new revelation. Description is useless, after such hasty inspection as we were able to give, and I shall not attempt it. If any reader wishes, he can find guide books and tales of travelers enough to satisfy his curiosity. And after all, if he should be so fortunate as to see these temples and those at Nikko, after having read the description, he will probably confess, as I do, that he had no conception of the reality.

Of quite another sort, and yet quite as important and

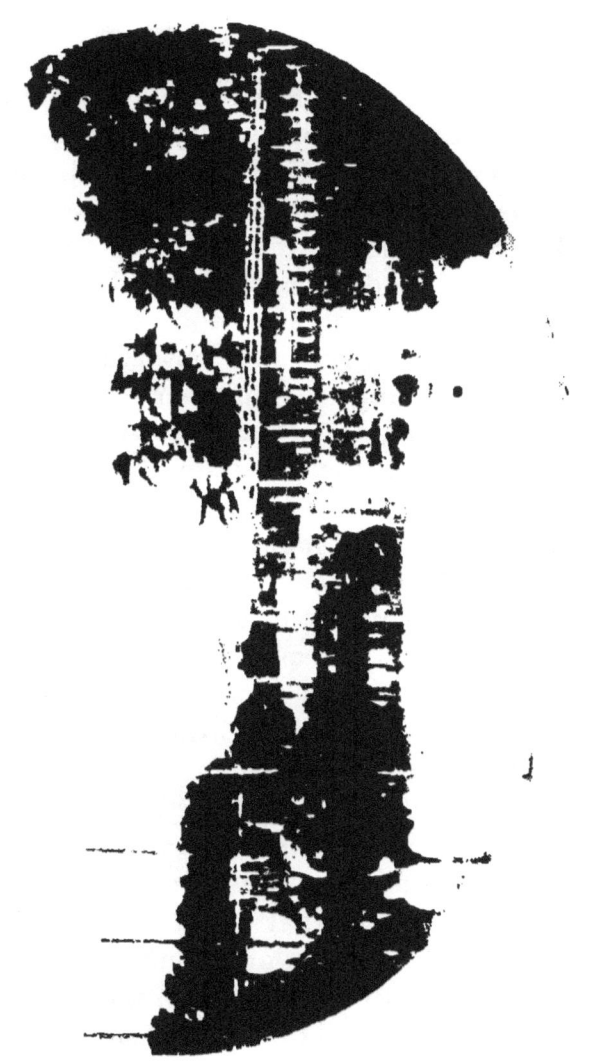

FUJIYAMA.—"THE PEERLESS."

interesting in its own way, is the great temple at Asakusa, another and distant quarter of the city, sacred to Kwannon, the goddess of Mercy. The images of this goddess which I have seen present the attractive face of a benignant and compassionate woman. The features are regular and graceful, and the eyes full of love and pity. One does not like to generalize too confidently from hasty and narrow premises and observations. But I cannot avoid the feeling that if there be degrees in idolatry, that of Japan, and even that of China, stands upon a higher level than that of India, if one may judge from the character of the images that meet his eye. The abominable distortions and monstrosities, the brutal display of lust and passion, so common and repulsive in India, seem largely wanting here. It may not be too much to ascribe, in part at least, to their different conceptions of their divinities, as expressed in their images, the greater cheerfulness and lightheartedness of the people which impresses one in Japan, as compared with those of India. The idolatry of India seems to rest down upon the people like an overshadowing and overwhelming pall of darkness and despair.

Stillness and peace reigned at Shiba. At Asakusa all was changed. Bustle and life prevailed. The immediate approach to the temple led through a paved avenue, lined on either side with shops. Here were displayed large stores of toys, confections, trinkets and fancy articles of many sorts. Troops of people, largely women and children, but with a plentiful sprinkling of men, filled the space between, going and coming, good-naturedly jostling one another, chatting and laughing and making holiday. The many colored dresses gave brightness to the picture. It is always holiday here, they tell us. On great fête days, of which there are a superabundance, the throngs are immense and wonderful.

Ours was only an ordinary day, yet a festive, holiday air was everywhere present. A large park-like enclosure encircles the temple, in which are booths for the sale of fancy articles and side-shows of many sorts, while seats and tea-houses in abundance provide rest and refreshment for the weary.

A two-storied gateway stands in front of the temple, with huge images of wood, one on either hand, the inevitable guardians of the gate. The bodies of these images, as of others in many places, were sprinkled with spit-balls of paper. This style of worship may not seem exactly complimentary, but there is no thought of disrespect. The spit-ball is a prayer, written upon a slip of paper, chewed and thrown at the idol. If the ball sticks, the prayer is heard. If it falls to the ground, the prayer falls with it. What proportion of prayers so addressed are successful we did not ascertain. The temple beyond is more than one hundred feet square, surrounded by a wide gallery or verandah, and surmounted by the heavy, curved and projecting roof which forms so picturesque a feature of the temples in Japan. The heavy projecting eaves and cornices are covered with wire netting to protect them from the flocks of doves which make the temple yard their home. Large columns of wood sunk in stone sockets, support the roof. Lanterns and pictures and votive offerings of many kinds are suspended on the pillars and from the ceiling. The sacred image, concealed from view, is placed behind a wire screen. For a consideration the inner apartment may be entered and the image itself, I believe, inspected. We did not make the investigation. Before it stands a huge money chest, with grating of parallel bars with sharply bevelled edges instead of a cover, into which intending worshippers cast their offerings. Clapping their hands to secure the attention of the divinity within, they kneel and pray or assume the attitude of prayer, undisturbed by the stream of idle or curious spectators. Their number must be great on ordinary days, and on feast days enormous. The revenue to the temple, through the money chest, though the amount of each offering be but small, must be correspondingly great.

At the right of the central shrine stands a wooden image of Binzuru, the helper of the sick, on whom Buddha is said to have conferred the power to heal all human maladies. Healing virtue is therefore ascribed to his image. It is elevated on a pedestal, but within easy reach of those who seek its aid. The afflicted come and rub their hands upon that part of the image answering to the portion of their own bodies in which their malady is supposed to lie—the eyes, the chest, the limbs, etc. The hand is then applied to the diseased part itself and the sufferer retires. So frequent and assiduous have been the applications that the features of the face are almost entirely obliterated, and the whole image worn as smooth as though highly polished. We half suspected that some laughing boys were making game of the idol as they went through the process of rubbing first its eyes and then their own. But the sight was one to evoke any other feeling than that of mirth, whether of pity, sorrow or disgust. Yet it would be hard to say in what particular such superstition differs from that which prompts thousands and tens of thousands of so-called Christians to make the pilgrimage, in hope of healing, to "Our Lady of Lourdes," or the "Holy Coat of Treves."

Close by the temple stands a high and, it must be confessed, very ugly tower of brick, which seems quite out of keeping with its surroundings. Its twelve stories rise to a height of three hundred and twenty feet. An electric elevator usually conveys aspirants to the eighth story, but, unfortunately, on this day was not in running order.

So we climbed slowly and wearily up the uncounted steps of the winding stairway, headed and followed by troops of schoolboys whose wooden clogs made music on the resounding boards, and whose bright eyes looked keenly and curiously at us. Emerging at the upper story we were rewarded by an extensive and magnificent view of Tokyo and the regions adjacent.

Descending, we regained our rikishas and took our way to Ueno Park, another of the popular resorts. Beautiful now, it must be specially so in the time of the cherry blossoms, which come in April, when its long avenue of cherry trees is one mass of bloom. Then all the populace assembles here to wonder and admire. Here was fought one of the bloody battles of the Revolution, and a monument commemorates the bravery and the fate of those who fell fighting for the Shogun. Here also, in mortuary temples similar to those of Nikko and Shiba, six of the Shoguns lie buried. These tombs we did not visit. Here, too, is the Museum, where we saw, in too rapid survey, specimens of the industrial arts and manufactures of Japan, both ancient and modern, antiquities from different parts of the Empire and historical relics of many kinds—clothing, armor, weapons and vehicles— exceedingly curious and interesting. Here, railed round and carefully guarded, by the side of one its avenues, stand the trees planted by General and Mrs. Grant at the time of their visit.

The Imperial University, with its extensive buildings, occupies the ground formerly belonging to the Yashiki, or town residence of the Daimio of Kaga. When Ieyasu chose Yedo for his capital, he required all the Daimios to reside six months in the city. Their residences, called Yashiki, covered large spaces of ground, with many buildings of various grades, for the accommodation of their families and their numerous retainers. A large portion of the city's territory was thus occupied. Since the abolition of the Daimiate, many of these yashikis have disappeared, some being destroyed by fire and others having been pulled down to make way for buildings and uses more suited to the needs of the new national and civic life. Some have been devoted to public uses, and among them that of the richest of them all, to the University. To this institution a peculiar interest attaches, for us, from the fact that its foundations were largely laid by representatives of the Reformed Church. Previous to the reorganization of the Government, Dr. Verbeck had carried on, at Nagasaki, a school of language which was largely attended by Samurai, or two-sworded men, of the powerful Satsuma clan. Some of these men became prominent in the new order of things, and summoned their former teacher to Tokyo. A school of language was organized by him and soon given entirely into his charge. For several years he acted as adviser of the Government in regard to educational matters. Out of this school of language, together with schools of medicine and engineering, grew the University of to-day, with its 120 instructors and more than 700 students in its five departments of Law, Medicine, Engineering, Literature and Science. With it have been connected, at different times during its earlier years, Dr. W. E. Griffis, the Rev. E. Warren Clark, Dr. David Murray, and others of the Reformed Church. At one time nearly or quite half the instructors were Americans. Of late years the number of foreign instructors has been diminishing, and, I believe, Americans have entirely disappeared.

Other large schools are to be found in Tokyo, to which I have briefly alluded in a former letter. Their presence causes a large influx of students from every part of the empire, numbering probably from 80,000 to 100,000.

They are among the most intelligent, active, restless and patriotic of the population. If their restlessness sometimes degenerates into turbulence, it is hardly to be wondered at. Young Japan is even more pronounced than Young America, and the cry, so common a short time ago, "Japan for the Japanese," has no more ardent advocates.

The "Church of Christ in Japan" is comparatively strong in Tokyo, numbering some twenty churches, with a membership, respectively, of from 40 to 400 and over, more than 3,400 in all. Many of their pastors are earnest, intelligent and devoted men, a few of whom it was my pleasure to meet. My great regret, which will be also lasting, was that I could not see all of them face to face and visit their churches, especially those with whose foundation and growth our own Mission has been more particularly identified

CHAPTER XXXIII.

KOBE, THE INLAND SEA AND NAGASAKI.

Tuesday, July 19th, found us again at sea on our way to Nagasaki. This was somewhat in the nature of a return trip, as our inability to stop there on our way up made it necessary to retrace our steps some seven hundred miles. But it would be impossible to leave Japan without visiting this point, of so much general and historic interest, and of such special importance to us as the centre of our South Japan Mission, and the seat of the "Steele Memorial College" and the "Sturges Seminary."

I must pass lightly over the details of the voyage—our brief stay at Kobe and the charming passage through the Inland Sea. At Kobe, a thriving city, with a large and growing trade, on the western shore of the Bay of Osaka, we had the unexpected pleasure of meeting all the members of the mission of the Southern Presbyterian Church, assembled at their annual meeting. The occasion that brought us into their society was a wedding, to which we were kindly invited. This is not an essential or ordinary element of a mission meeting. But so long as missionaries are but men and women, and not angels, they may be expected to marry and be given in marriage, and such occasions bring as much pleasure and blessedness on mission ground as on any other. Into the brightness of this it was a pleasure to be admitted, and to meet so large, so happy, so devoted and so hopeful a company of laborers in the Lord's vineyard in Japan. In fact, whatever may be the peculiar difficulties and special preplexities and problems of the work in Japan at the present time, I have yet to meet the first missionary who does not take, on the whole, a hopeful view of the situation, and especially of the future of the Church and Kingdom of Christ in this Empire.

Members of other missions, also, were present, among them Miss Y. May King, M.D., who was for a short time connected with our Mission at Amoy. Miss King is now a member of the Southern Methodist (U. S.) Mission at Kobe, has a home and dispensary here, and is doing an excellent work. She hopes ere long to have a hospital also provided, and so to be enabled to enlarge her sphere of activity and usefulness. At her hospitable table we were privileged to dine, the following evening, with Bishop Key of the Southern M. E. Church, on a tour similar to our own, but in the opposite direction. It was part of his errand at Kobe to organize a conference, and his whole soul seemed filled with enthusiasm by what he has seen of the work. He had come directly from home to Japan, proposing to go on to China and India, and thus spend a year. "But I have seen so much already," said he, "that I feel like giving up the rest and going back immediately to stir up the churches at home." The feeling has doubtless grown upon him since—as he has gone from field to field, from land to land—of the utter disproportion between the forces furnished by the churches and actually engaged, and the work that waits. It cannot but grow in the heart of any true believer in Christ, and in the intent and authority of His last command, who comes into contact with the multitudes in these Eastern lands, who looks with sympathy and pity on their condition without the Gospel, sees what that Gospel has already done among them, and realizes how wide open is the door and how great the need for larger efforts.

Of the passage through the Inland Sea it is difficult to speak in terms of measured soberness. It is enchanting. The sea, inlocked between the large islands of Nippon and Shikoku, is thickly studded with countless islands and islets, some high and mountainous, some wild and rocky, some crowned with forests, some cultivated, terrace above terrace, from shore to summit. Numerous fishing and other villages dot the shores. Small steamers ply among the islands, and innumerable fishing-boats and sailing craft dot the bosom of the land-locked bays. All day long, from dawn till dark, we sailed through this scene of enchantment, through passages sometimes so narrow that one could almost toss a biscuit to shore on either hand, and on the forecastle the crew stood ready at any moment to drop the anchor should anything go wrong. The tide runs so strong that vessels are sometimes turned completely round. The changes were so constant, and the rapidly unfolding beauty so great and varied, that the eye never wearied of gazing, and it was hard to leave the deck. Let no one fail, who visits Japan, to sail the Inland Sea.

We had expected to be in Nagasaki by Saturday evening. But midnight of Friday found us at Shimonoseki, where we lay at anchor till daylight, and then spent four hours taking in coal. Emerging from the western mouth of the Shimonoseki Strait, the rising wind and falling barometer admonished us of the presence of a typhoon outside. So all day, till three or four in the afternoon, we lay under the shelter of a large island and escaped its fury, though the sea into which we then put out was rough enough. It was Sunday morning when we cast anchor in Nagasaki harbor, and received the warm welcome of the brethren there. Their houses, and the schools, are picturesquely perched on the sides of a steep bluff which overlooks the town and harbor. Steep stairways of stone, or paved inclines of easier grade, lead up to the higher levels. The views, when the height is gained, are beautiful in the extreme. The harbor is long, sinuous and not very wide, resembling, somewhat, a section of the Hudson in its most beautiful portion. High hills, densely wooded, with numerous bays and indentations, shut it in on either side. At its entrance lies the singular, conical-shaped island of Pappenberg, seeming to stand guard against unwelcome intruders. The foreign settlement, with its business and offices, stands on the flat below, while the homes of the foreign residents, merchants, etc., seek the slopes and summits of the hills. Beyond it, on the shore, is the island Deshima, to which, in former times, the few Dutch merchants who were allowed to reside here, were confined. Some of the houses they occupied are still standing, and in use for purposes of trade. The native town stretches along the shore for miles, and up the valleys between the hills, a compact mass of low houses teeming with human life. Upon the water numerous steamers, large and small, lay at anchor, with junks and small boats innumerable. The arrival and departure of the former and the movements of the latter gave animation to the scene. The view at night, when every vessel bore its lantern, and hundreds of lights glimmered below, seeming to rival in multitude the stars in the heaven above, was like a glimpse of fairyland. Prominent among the shipping were the vessels composing the Asiatic squadron of our own navy, each with the Stars and Stripes floating from the peak. It was a welcome sight to exiles far from home. A Russian man-of-war, far larger and more formidable looking, lay just below them. It was a grateful sound and graceful compliment when a day or two later, as she left the port, her band played "Hail Columbia!"

Needless to say that all these observations were not made that early Sunday morning. Escorted by Messrs. Stout and Pieters and Miss Lanterman, we left the good ship "Kobe Maru," and climbed the hill to the hospitable homes that had so long waited to receive us. Thence, after breakfast, to the morning service in the native church, where some words would certainly be expected from the new-comer. These he was glad to give, though upon such short notice, and also to baptize two infant children, the sons of Pastor Segawa and Principal Ohgimi of "Steele." The absence of the scholars of both schools made a sensible difference in the size of the congregation. Yet it was cheering to meet the brethren of the church, its permanent representatives among the thousands and tens of thousands of this large city. It has been hard soil here to cultivate in the past. But a brighter day seems to have dawned already, for the Church in Nagasaki and in all the region dependent upon it.

For nine years, from 1859, Dr. Verbeck alone represented the Reformed Church here. No direct missionary work, could then be done, but the foundation for future work both here and elsewhere, by himself and others, were faithfully laid. Here, too, some of the first and most notable converts were gathered and baptized by him. The history of missions contains few more interesting and thrilling stories than that of the discovery of a new testament floating on the water by Wakasa, and his subsequent conversion to Christ through its instrumentality.

For more than nine years longer, I believe, the post was occupied alone by Mr. Stout. What one man could do he did. But if the work grew slowly, the Church itself was largely responsible by with holding the help for which he plead so long and earnestly. In later years help has been given, though not yet according to the need, and now three missionary families and the two flourishing boarding-schools for boys and girls, with three churches and twenty-six outstations, represent the strength and, in some measure, the results of this Mission, and its claim upon the sympathy, the prayers and the further aid of the Church.

The "Steele School" or "College," as it is proposed to call it, has a fine building finely located on the southern spur of the hill of which I have already spoken. This building, as is known to many, was the gift of the Rev. Dr. Steele, for many years the President of our Board of Foreign Missions, in perpetual memory of his son, Wm. H. Steele, Jr. Its wide hall, commodious chapel and recitation and lecture rooms, admirably adapt it for the purpose for which it was designed. The dormitories, in Japanese style, the kitchen and dining-room, and other adjuncts of the school, form a much humbler edifice in the rear. The front is unobstructed, commands a noble view of the harbor, and is open to every breeze—a matter of great importance in such a climate as this. Another building still, contains a few sleeping apartments and a fine gymnasium, which is also used for public entertainments and commencement exercises. The great need of the school at present is larger accommodation for boarders, experience showing that this class is much more desirable and fuller of promise than a like number of day-scholars. By a somewhat recent change in the plan of conduct the Rev. M. Ohgimi, well-known to many in the Church at home, has been placed at the head of the institution. He has entered upon his duties with zeal and discretion, and the arrangement has thus far proved eminently satisfactory. Connected with the grounds occupied by the school is space sufficient for another house, which it is hoped may some day be erected for the occupancy of the missionary who may teach in the school.

Proceeding northward we reach the house occupied by Mr. Oltmans and his growing family, which should come down and be replaced before it tumbles in on their heads. Thence, still northward, a short walk brings us to Mr. Stout's, and passing this a few steps only we come to the Sturges Seminary. Its grounds immediately adjoin those of Mr. Stout, and, though on a slightly lower level, they are still raised far above the street, to which a high stone wall descends and a steep flight of stone steps leads down. The original building stands almost on the edge of a precipice. It contains pleasant rooms for the accommodation of the ladies in charge, for recitation and for sleeping apartments for a small number of scholars. The new building, added two years ago, supplies rooms for a much larger number, all finished and furnished in Japanese style and captivating in their simple neatness. Of this school, also, a Japanese gentleman, Mr. Saito, has been made principal, with happy results. It was gratifying to learn that, while mission schools for girls generally throughout the Empire have to deplore a decline in the number of scholars, the number in attendance on "Sturges" is steadily increasing. We found Miss Lanterman looking forward with bright anticipations to the coming year—anticipations that have been abundantly verified so far as the school is concerned, but which she, alas! was not permitted to realize. It lends, and will always lend, a shade of peculiar sadness to the memory of our brief visit, that she who seemed so bright and full of earnest purpose should have been called away so soon.

We were assured that our delay in coming had been a grievous disappointment to the scholars of both these schools, as it certainly was to us, however unavoidable.

They had entered with zest into hearty preparations for a rousing Japanese welcome. It would have been a happy thing to see them. But we were too late. None of the girls remained, and we saw only a few lads who preferred to remain and study during the vacation rather than return to their homes. But the principals and teachers of the two schools, together with Pastor Segawa, invited us to a regular Japanese dinner, an invitation which I alone was able to accept. It was given in one of the best native restaurants, or tea-houses, at some distance from the mission houses. The spot was beautifully chosen, half-way up the hillside, under the shade of noble trees, the whole front open to the south, whence came a refreshing breeze. There, seated on the floor, with shoes removed — the smooth mats scrupulously clean — we passed two pleasant hours. Course after course was brought in in lacquered trays—largely of fish of various kinds and in various styles of preparation, from raw fish in thin slices, to baked and boiled and broiled—the whole culminating, according to custom, in bowls of rice. But the viands were the least interesting part of the entertainment. Though the only American present, and utterly innocent of any knowledge of Japanese, I found Messrs. Ohgimi and Segawa such adepts in English that conversation was easy with them, and through them with the others, and the hours passed swiftly. Indeed it was necessary to cut short the time one would have been glad to spend in such association and surroundings, in order to take the steamer which was to bear us back to Kobe.

I had meant to speak of other pleasures enjoyed at Nagasaki, especially of the delightful evenings, and of visits, one with Mr. Stout to the house of a dear, old English lady, Mrs. Goodall, who has a home for girls, maintained at her own charges, where she trains them under her own eye to be useful Christian women—a most blessed work, and sure to have its blessed rewards, of one with Mr. Oltmans to the U. S. S. "Lancaster," where it was a pleasure to meet three Christian officers ; and of another with Messrs. Oltmans and Pieters and their families to Pappenberg, the island famed as the spot where thousands of Christians, more than two centuries ago, were hurled from the summit to the rocks and the sea beneath, "for the testimony of Jesus." We climbed to the summit, and found it hard to believe the truth of the story. In fact, I believe there is no record anywhere written to confirm it. But the tradition will doubtless always hang around the spot.

CHAPTER XXXIV.

KYOTO THE WESTERN CAPITAL AND MISHIMA.

Our stay in Nagasaki was all too short. The work in Kiu Shiu was for many years slow, hard and discouraging, the people showing themselves peculiarly bigoted and unsusceptible, even when not hostile, to the truth. Of late years a marked change has taken place, and, perhaps, few regions in Japan have offered more encouragement in proportion to the amount of effort expended on the work of evangelization. It would have been a pleasure and a privilege to visit Saga and other outstations more remote, and see something of the field occupied by the mission, and the results of labor, as well as some of the natural features and beauties of the island. But necessity forbade, and regrets were useless.

Nothing can ever mar or obliterate the impression of the preeminent beauty of Nagasaki and its surroundings among all the stations we visited. We counted our good friends happy in having their lot cast amid such delightful scenes, and left them with the prayer that the beauty of the Lord our God might also be upon them, and the work of their hands even more abundantly established.

The good ship "Verona" received us on the afternoon of July 27th, and, farewells exchanged, we were soon steaming down the harbor, rounding Pappenberg and standing out to sea, our faces set for Kobe, Yokohama, and home. At Kobe we left the steamer for overland journey by rail, and were met by Mr. Ballagh, who had kindly come down to act as escort to Yokohama. Here, also, we were so fortunate as to fall in with Dr. T. Romeyn Beck and his good wife, formerly of Hope College. The doctor has for several years been engaged in teaching in the high school in Yamaguchi, and seems to have been remarkably successful in winning the confidence and good will of the school authorities and the people. The contracts with him have been repeatedly renewed, and a building provided in which he is allowed to hold Bible classes, and impart religious instruction. Without delaying at Kobe we proceeded the same morning by rail to Kyoto.

This city, called also Sai Kyo, or the Western Capital, is the "sacred city" of Japan. Here for a thousand years the Mikado, Son of Heaven, held his court religiously secluded from the sight of, and contact with, the people of whom he was the ostensible ruler. Hence, when restored to actual sovereignty, he removed his court to Tokyo. The situation is well chosen and beautiful with surrounding and overshadowing mountains. The palace grounds are extensive, in the heart of the city, but closed from public view. Temples great and small abound, some of them of great size and magnificence. It is the centre and stronghold of Buddhist faith and propagandism, having more than 3,000 Buddhist temples and 8,000 priests. Foreigners were for a long time rigorously excluded. There was pointed out to us, as the train neared the station, the walls of an extensive school for Buddhist priests, a theological seminary in fact, in which the Bible is said to be used as a text book, and where destructive criticism of the Book of books may be supposed to have full course. It is noted also for its manufactures, and purchasers of such things are fascinated and go wild over the stores of embroidery, porcelain, and goods and curios of various sorts that are here displayed. Its streets are broad, laid out at right angles with methodical exactness and kept scrupulously clean, while large public squares afford ample breathing space. In many respects it is the most attractive and interesting city in Japan.

Nor is it less interesting as a centre of missionary operations. For here is the most important station of the American Board in the Empire, with its noble company of missionaries and the famed Doshisha University, with which the name of Joseph Neesima will be forever inseparably connected.

The American Presbyterian Church (North), and the Protestant Episcopal Church of North America have also each a station here. We were not so fortunate as to find any of the missionaries of the American Board in their homes. It was vacation time and all were scattered to their summer retreats among the hills, but Brother Porter, of the Presbyterian Mission, kindly conducted us through the city, and Brother Gring, of the Episcopal Mission, hospitably entertained us for the night.

The "Doshisha," though not properly an institution of the American Board, was established and has grown to its present proportions under its fostering care. A goodly number of its instructors are missionaries of that Board. The title "Doshisha," meaning "One Purpose Company," has no reference to the character of the institution, but simply to the organization or corporation formed by Mr. Neesima and others for the purpose of establishing it. Begun in 1875 with many misgivings and many discouragements, it has had a remarkable growth. Friends have been raised up for it in America and in Japan, large sums have been given for purposes of endowment, purchase of land and erection of buildings, while the two teachers and eight pupils of 1875 have increased to a faculty of forty, with more than 500 students in 1892. As we visited the grounds lying north of the palace grounds, and inspected the imposing array of buildings substantially built of brick, recitation halls, Science Hall, Chapel and Library (on another square), and saw the excavations in progress for the erection of still another, Divinity Hall, it was hard to know which most to admire, the wisdom and faith that had wrought to secure such tangible results or the blessing of God which has attended them.

It was hard also to repress a wish that friends might be found in the churches represented in work for the (United) "Church of Christ in Japan," the Presbyterian and Reformed Churches in America, who would make like generous provision for the efficiency and permanent establishment of the Meiji Gakuin at Tokyo. The needs are as great, the field of influence certainly as wide, if not wider, and the promise to faith and liberality as encouraging in Tokyo as here. In fact, as Tokyo is now the political and educational centre of Japan, it would seem to be the place, of all others, for a well endowed, thoroughly equipped and thoroughly Christian University.

To the eastward of the city, shutting it in and overlooking it, is a range of hills crowded with temples, some of them of great age and magnificence, and with abodes of numerous priests. Some of the principal of these temples we saw, the Buddhist Chion-in the Shinto Gion and Kiomidzu. I would like to describe them and their surroundings but time and space forbid. Of the first, which was also the largest and handsomest, we were told that it was very heavily mortgaged and in danger of being sold. This fate has overtaken many of the temples in Kyoto of late years, through the falling off in revenue, so that now it is said there are 300 less than a few years ago. But the decline in popular interest and faith which this seems to show may be offset by the Higashi Hongwanji temple now in process of erection in another part of the city. We saw it the next day, the only really new temple we did see in Japan. It is immense and magnificent. Ten years and millions of dollars have been spent in building it. It was to have been finished in 1892, but is far from complete. It has been the object of widespread popular interest and contribution. On the broad verandah or colonade which encompasses it lay, in large coils, the cables made of women's hair contributed in a spirit of devotion, with which the huge timbers used for pillars, frames and rafters were hauled from the forests and hoisted to their place. Twenty-nine such cables, a little hand bill informed us, had been worn out in the process, while twenty-four remain still intact. How many women must have sacrificed that which is everywhere regarded as one of her greatest adornments, that this house might be built. "The glory of a woman is her hair," and nowhere is this more true than in Japan.

Characteristic of this multitude of temples, as elsewhere also, are the temple bells. In the enclosure of the Chion-in hung one of the largest, 10.8 feet in height, nine feet in diameter, $9\frac{1}{2}$ inches thick, and weighing more than seventy tons. It hung suspended in a wooden tower distinct from the temple itself. These bells are rung, not with a metal clapper as with us, but by the swinging against them of a stick of timber suspended outside and operating like a battering ram.

The sound is therefore softened and free from metallic clangor, and the soft prolonged resonance of the bells is remarkable, and delightful to the ear. Few experiences have been more charming than the tones of these innumerable bells in the early morning of the next day, blending in sweetest harmony and filling the air with their tremulous vibrations. It was like being roused from sleep by the "music of the spheres."

Shrill, strident and discordant, a noisy steam whistle broke in upon the music and murdered it and sleep together. So discordant and repulsive, I dare say, in the estimation of many has the civilization of which the steam whistle is one of the most characteristic voices, broken in upon the repose of ages in this island empire.

From Kyoto to Nagoya our course lay next, to spend the Sabbath in the latter. On the way thither we passed through the region devastated by the earthquake of October 1891. The wide extent and terrible effects of that catastrophe place it among the most destructive of such convulsions in the annals of the world. Many traces of it still remained in heaps of ruins, roofs of houses propped upon timbers for temporary shelter, buildings in process of restoration and the like.

Yet it was surprising to find how far the work of recovery had gone. Doubtless this was more evident along the railway than in the interior districts. Yet one could not fail to be impressed with the marks of energy and hope displayed after a disaster that seemed fitted to crush out hope and energy together. Nagoya itself, though removed somewhat from the centre of disturbance, suffered severely, and the tales told us of ruin, danger and escape were thrilling indeed. Of all the calamities to which men are exposed there would seem to be none more appalling than this. A slight shock in the middle of our first night served as a reminder of what had been, and a suggestion of what might be. It was sufficient.

Out of the calamity, as so often happens in the providence of God, good has resulted. The self-denying labors, the quickly extended aid and sympathy of Christian people, native and foreign, did much to break down prejudice and open the way for the Gospel. One of the most touching and Christlike fruits we saw in the orphanage established here for children, whose parents perished in that awful time. It is a branch of the work begun by Mr. Ishii at Okayama. Mr. Ishii is a most remarkable man, who seems as truly called of God to work of this sort, and to have been as distinctly guided and blessed by Him in it, as George Muller, of Bristol, England. His work is conducted on the same principles of prayer and faith, and many are the instances of striking interpositions on its behalf in answer to prayer. We found more than forty little ones in the orphanage at Nagoya, under a man who seemed every way likeminded with his principal. His sympathy with the children and their confidence in him were evident and touching.

On Sabbath morning we worshipped with the congregation connected with the Southern Presbyterian Mission. The Rev. R. E. McAlpine, Mr. Ballagh's son-in-law, is stationed here and has charge of the work. The M. E. Mission is well represented here, also, and in the afternoon a union meeting was held in their commodious church, at which, by invitation, I had the pleasure of making the principal address. Few things are more delightful on mission ground than the spirit of sympathy and fellowship which prevails among workers of almost every denomination. May that spirit never be less. After service we went to call on Mr. Higashi, one of the earliest, if not the very earliest, Christians here. Unfortunately the old gentleman was away from home. His dwelling is on the outskirts of the town, and quite humble in appearance, of low rooms and narrow passages leading out upon a garden. It was quite characteristic that the old lady, our absent friend's wife, received us modestly and with no word of apology, though stripped to the waist, and engaged in washing her grandchildren in the bath tub. It was equally significant of the change which had come over the spirit of royalty to be told that the Emperor himself was once entertained in this humble home.

The next day found us at Shidzuoka where we passed the night. Much of the day was spent in searching for a more desirable location for the pastor, and meeting place for the little company of believers. It enabled us to make quite the circuit of this old castle town, visit its most noted temple, and pass, though we did not enter, the spot where the last Shogun dwells in peaceful retirement, "far from the madding crowd," and the strife of court and camp. In the evening the church members met with us at the home of Pastor Ito. It illustrated the patience of these brethren that they listened attentively to the secretary (and his interpreter) for an hour, and then to Brother Ballagh independently for another thirty minutes.

We rose at four the next morning, and by 5.15 were on our way, with Pastor Ito in company, to Numadzu and Mishima. We reached the latter place after an hour's ride in rikishas at 7.45. Here is the building once a saki brewery, now transformed into a school and church by the generous gift of one of the Christians of the place, Mr. Hanajima. The seats are made from the old saki casks or vats, a number of which, still in existence, but dry and dusty, we saw through a small door in the rear of the church, in an apartment appropriately dark. Here in the upper story Miss Lizzie Ballagh has lived for years, the only foreigner in the town, conducting a school for girls. It is a lonely and self-sacrificing position, its only rewards to be found in the consciousness of serving the Lord—and in the influence exerted for good on the lives of her pupils.

Mishima is famed for its beauty, its abundant springs gushing free, cold and clear from the earth and amid rocks, forming when united a considerable stream, and for its Shinto temple. It adds to its laurels a visit from General Grant. We followed humbly in his footsteps and saw the objects on which his eyes rested, little changed since then. The same pool—filled with carp and gold fish, some of them of immense size—boiled like a pot with their motions when food was thrown to them. The same huge temple court, overshadowed by great trees, swarmed with flocks of pigeons and barn-yard fowl, and in the temple, perhaps, the same priest was performing his worship in behalf of two suppliants who knelt and bowed behind him, clapping his hands, waving a bunch of paper streamers and prostrating himself before the various shrines.

Thence returning to Numadzu, we took train for Gotemba, skirting the base of Fujiyama, "peerless" always, but coyly hiding her peerlessness in masses of cloud reaching half-way down. To Gotemba many residents of Yokohama come for the summer, weary of the heat. The eye is soothed by masses of living green, and rests on prospects of surpassing beauty, while the cooler air gives vigor to the enfeebled frame. Here again we met a little company of faithful ones, as well as some missionary friends, and spoke to them of the things of the Kingdom. Here, too, Brother Ballagh forsook me to make his way with a party of friends to the summit of Fuji, while I made mine to Yokohama through scenes of beauty, mountain, vale and sea, which I do not dare attempt to describe.

HEATHEN TEMPLE.—MISHIMA.

CHAPTER XXXV.

LAST LOOK AT YOKOHAMA.

It would be a shame to take leave of Japan without a few words more concerning Yokohama. Not specially interesting in itself, perhaps, it has yet a special interest by reason of its connection with the beginnings of the Mission work which is now so widely extended through the empire, and also by reason of that which still centres and is carried on in it. The "first things" were found and done here in a remarkable degree.

When Drs. Hepburn and Brown first came to Japan, Yokohama had no existence, save as a small fishing village, yet here the negotiations were held and the interchange of national gifts and communications, by Com. Perry, which resulted in the opening of Japan. In 1861, or thereabout, it became the place of foreign residence, merchant, missionary and others, instead of Kanagawa, across the bay, where they at first resided. Here Dr. Brown pursued with others the work of translation of the scriptures, with which his name will be inseparably linked, and of which he was permitted to see the completion, so far as the New Testament is concerned, before his death. Here, too, he gathered and carried forward that class of young men from whom were drawn not only some of the earliest converts and members of the church but also some of its best and most faithful preachers and pastors of to-day.

Here, in 1864, the first convert, so far as known, Yano Riu, was baptized in secret by Mr. Ballagh, and the first Protestant church organized by him with eleven members in 1872. It was organized as, and styled, a "Union Church," as if in unconscious prophecy of that larger union which has since been formed, of all the Presbyterian and Reformed churches and workers, called at first the "Union Church of Christ," and now simply the "Church of Christ in Japan," with its 72 churches and 10,862 members, its 6 Classes, or Presbyteries, and its Synod. The old mother church, the "Kaigan," of Yokohama, still retains not only historical but numerical pre-eminence, having a membership of nearly or quite 700. This year it celebrated the twentieth anniversary of its foundation, an occasion of peculiar interest, at which, however, it was not my privilege to be present. But I was privileged, on the second Sunday of my stay, to attend the morning service in the fine large church, erected under Mr. Ballagh's supervision, listen to a sermon by Pastor Inagaki, and then sit with him and his people at the table of the Lord. The number of communicants was large, and as the eye and heart embraced them, and the mind traveled back to the small beginnings, only twenty years ago, it was impossible to resist the profound impression of what God had already wrought, and how widely and effectually He had opened the door of the faith to these dwellers in this island empire, nor the equally profound conviction that that door never can be shut.

A peculiar interest attaches to this church building, from the fact that $1,000 was contributed by Christian natives of Hawaii, or the Sandwich Islands, and used in its erection. By a happy arrangement with the Japanese church, it is used every Sabbath, immediately after the dispersion of the native congregation, for an English service by the Union Church. This church is composed of foreigners of various nationalities and church affiliations, and has a considerable membership, with an able and acceptable pastor, the Rev. Dr. Meacham, of Canada. As he was then at home in Canada, we did not have the pleasure of meeting him. But I heard much that was excellent of his influence and work. Such a church and such a pastor must be a power for good among the foreign residents, self-exiled from their homes, and removed both from the helps and from the restraints to which they have been accustomed. It is a sad fact, to which I have referred before, that the lives of many so-called Christians in foreign ports reflect anything but honor on the name they bear. It is not too much to say of them, in the strong language of Scripture, that the name of Christ is blasphemed among the heathen because of them. Among them originate and freely circulate those stories of the idle, useless lives and unworthy character of missionaries, which are poured into the ears of new comers or of travelers upon the decks of steamers. Bandied from mouth to mouth they grow more and more distorted and untruthful, till the hearer is amazed and then bewildered, or even, perhaps, convinced. The best correction is contact with the missionaries themselves and with their work. In that presence they cannot live a day.

In no field of missionary effort, probably, has the work of female education assumed a higher form or been productive of greater good than in Japan. The beginnings of that work were made in Yokohama. I have before spoken of our own Ferris Seminary and need not here repeat. It was a pleasure to visit the " Home " of the Woman's Union Missionary Society, located on the bluff not very far from Ferris. Begun by Mrs. Pruyn, and for many years conducted by Mrs. Pierson and Miss Crosby with faithful assistants, it has proved a truly Christian home, "home of the soul," as well, to a large number of Japan's fair daughters both of pure and mixed blood. Connected with it is a Woman's School for the training of Christian women for Christian work, under the special charge of Mrs. Pierson, who is, herself, an indefatigable evangelist.

One interesting incident of our stay in this city was a visit we paid one morning to a day school presided over by Miss Case, of the Presbyterian Board, in the midst of the native city. Its pupils, boys and girls, number about 300, and are drawn from the lower classes of the people, though each pays something for instruction. It occupies the old Sumiyoshi Cho Church building, that body having been transferred to the fine brick structure, with tall spire, known as Shiloh Church, and erected through the instrumentality, and largely, I believe, through the liberality, of Dr. Hepburn. The attendance at the school was large, though smaller than usual on account of the prevalence of measles. It was a pleasing sight to see the scholars, who were playing when we arrived, march into the assembly room with ordered step and take their places. A native air was sung, the teacher, a young Japanese woman, beating time to the music with thin boards struck together after the manner of cymbals. This was followed by a Christian hymn and the repetition in concert of I. Corinthians xiii. and the Lord's Prayer. The children looked happy and joined heartily in all these exercises, moved thereto, perhaps, more by the presence and approving smile of Dr. and Mrs. Hepburn, well-known friends who have taken a deep interest in the school, than of unknown strangers.

It was a rare pleasure to meet these honored and beloved servants of Christ and Japan, whose coming antedated, by some weeks, the arrival of Dr. and Mrs. Brown. At an interview in their own house I was surprised to learn that Dr. Hepburn had been with David Abeel at Amoy fifty years ago, and delighted to hear his reminiscences of that early period of missionary effort in China, of the whole marvellous development of the work in that Empire, and the latter, but even more marvellous growth in Japan, of which he had been a witness, and of the latter an important part. His dictionary has laid missionaries and foreigners in Japan under lasting obligation, and his medical skill, evangelical kindly spirit and blameless life, have won for him and for the truths he represented a place in multitudes of hearts.

"Doctor," said I, "if you can possibly put yourself back again at Amoy with Abeel, and then look forward in imagination, could you have then conceived it possible that the progress you have yourself witnessed would have been made in fifty years, in your own lifetime?"

"It would have been inconceivable," was his reply. Nor is it possible, now, to conceive whereunto the Church of Christ in these lands will grow in the next fifty years. The blessing of God upon the comparatively small effort put forth—small when compared with the vastness of the multitudes to be evangelized, and of the resources which the church in Christian lands has at command for their evangelization—is promise as real as any recorded in Holy Writ of what may be expected when the church shall truly obey the prophetic injunction: "Arise, shine, for thy light is come, and the glory of the Lord is risen upon thee." No conviction is stronger or more deeply lodged in my mind than this, that the triumphs already won for and by the Gospel in these Eastern lands, and the open door of access to their waiting and perishing millions, constitute God's challenge to His church and add new emphasis to the Redeemer's last command.

No mention of Yokohama would be complete without allusion to the many glimpses, under varying conditions, but all of singular beauty, of the stately snow-crowned head of Fujiyama. When sailing up and down the coast, or even when approaching it by land, skirting its very base, impenetrable clouds had shut it from our sight. But many a charming vision was granted us during our stays at Yokohama. At early morning, reflecting back the rays of rising day, its sunny masses all aglow with light, in the clear noonday or the fading light and glowing color of the setting sun, its shapely summit stood above the hills that intervened, an object of beauty and impressiveness never to be forgotten. One ceases to wonder at the passion for it cherished by the natives of the land it adorns and glorifies. We came to love the sight and look for it with wonder and admiration somewhat akin to theirs. And when, at last, we had taken leave of the dear friends with whom we had spent so many happy days and weeks, and had already left them far behind on our homeward way across the sea, while the evening shadows gathered and the lower land had sunk from sight beneath the sea, there, above the clouds, appeared the well-known summit, and from it, just as we would have wished, we received our last farewell.

www.ingramcontent.com/pod-product-compliance
Lightning Source LLC
Chambersburg PA
CBHW031956230426
43672CB00010B/2168